*Jews
and Catholics
Together*

Jews and Catholics Together

CELEBRATING THE LEGACY OF *NOSTRA AETATE*

EDITED BY **MICHAEL ATTRIDGE**

NOVALIS

© 2007 Novalis, Saint Paul University, Ottawa, Canada

Cover Photo: Jupiter Images
Layout: Christiane Lemire and Audrey Wells

Business Offices:
Novalis Publishing Inc.
10 Lower Spadina Avenue, Suite 400
Toronto, Ontario, Canada
M5V 2Z2
Phone: 1-800-387-7164
Fax: 1-800-204-4140
E-mail: books@novalis.ca
www.novalis.ca

Novalis Publishing Inc.
4475 Frontenac Street
Montréal, Québec, Canada
H2H 2S2

Library and Archives Canada Cataloguing in Publication

Jews and Catholics together : celebrating the legacy of Nostra aetate / edited by Michael Attridge.

Includes bibliographical references.
ISBN 978-2-89507-840-1

1. Catholic Church–Relations–Judaism. 2. Judaism–Relations–Catholic Church. 3. Vatican Council (2nd : 1962-1965). Declaratio de ecclesiae habitudine ad religiones non-Christianas. I. Attridge, Michael, 1967-

BM535.J468 2007   261.2'6   C2007-900415-6

Printed in Canada.

All rights reserved. No part of this publication may be reproduced, stored in a retrieval system, or transmitted in any form, or by any means, electronic, mechanical, photocopying, recording, or otherwise, without the written permission of the publisher.

We acknowledge the financial support of the Government of Canada through the Book Publishing Industry Development Program (BPIDP) for our publishing activities.

5 4 3 2 1   11 10 09 08 07

Contents

Introduction — *Michael Attridge* 7

1. *Nostra aetate*: Forty Years Later — *George H. Tavard* ... 13
2. Jewish-Catholic Relations from *Nostra aetate* to the Present — *Ovey N. Mohammed* 48
3. *Nostra aetate* and *Dabru Emet* — *David Novak* 72
4. Issues for Future Catholic-Jewish Relations — *Edward Idris Cardinal Cassidy* 90
5. Issues Facing Christian-Jewish Dialogue — *Rabbi Riccardo Di Segni* 122
6. Finding a Place for the Other: Challenges Facing the Future of Jewish-Christian Dialogue — *James F. Puglisi*. 131

Afterword — *Gregory Baum* 149

Appendix: Questions Concerning the Jews: Proposals from the Secretariat for Christian Unity, November 1961 166

INTRODUCTION

The year 2005 was one of great celebration for Jews and Catholics. In cities throughout the world, universities, ecumenical commissions, and interreligious bodies commemorated the most remarkable step taken in relations between these two faith communities in almost 2,000 years. The reason for the festivities was the fortieth anniversary of *Nostra aetate*, a document promulgated in 1965 by the Roman Catholic Church's Second Vatican Council, which entirely renovated the Church's teachings on Judaism and the Jewish people. After Vatican II, Jews were no longer accused of deicide, or "God-killing." Instead, the Church taught that "what happened in the suffering and death of Christ cannot be blamed upon all the Jews living then or upon the Jews today" (*Nostra aetate*, 4). It spoke with admiration of the Jewish people as "the root of the good olive tree" who "still remain most dear to God ... for God does not repent of the gifts he makes nor of the calls he issues" (cf. Rom 11:28-29). *Nostra aetate* was a profound change in the Church's teaching; this fortieth anniversary year was a time to remember this extraordinary document, to recall the progress made in further relations over the past four decades, and to look with great hope to the future.

In Toronto, the University of St. Michael's College was the venue for a day-long symposium bringing together six internationally distinguished Jewish and Catholic scholars. George Tavard, a theological adviser at Vatican II, began the day by recalling the intriguing history of *Nostra aetate*, including an early draft of the document that never made it to the council floor. Professors Ovey Mohammed and David Novak continued by marking the milestones in relations between these two communities over the past forty years: with Mohammed focusing on five official documents of the Catholic Church and Novak attending to the Jewish equivalent of *Nostra aetate*, entitled *Dabru Emet*, published in 2000. The remaining three presentations addressed challenges and opportunities for Jews and Catholics as we journey together into tomorrow, offered by three prominent religious leaders: Cardinal Edward Idris Cassidy, President Emeritus of the Vatican's Pontifical Council for Promoting Christian Unity and Commission for Religious Relations with the Jews; Rabbi Riccardo Di Segni, the Chief Rabbi in Rome, the oldest Jewish settlement in the Western world; and the Very Reverend James Puglisi, SA, Minister General of the Franciscan Friars of the Atonement.

Jews and Catholic Together: Celebrating the Legacy of Nostra aetate is the result of this event. In addition to reproducing here the papers of the symposium, I am delighted to include two additional contributions. First is an Afterword by the world-renowned Canadian theologian Gregory Baum, an adviser to the Secretariat for Christian Unity during the Second Vatican Council and an expert in Jewish-Catholic relations. His essay provides an excellent and insightful summary of the other contributions and deserves to be read twice: once at the beginning and again at the end. Second is the previously unpublished first draft of *Nostra aetate,* entitled *Quæstiones de Judaeis* ("Questions Concerning the Jews"), to which Tavard refers in his text. It should be noted that although the final text of *Nostra aetate* deals with many world religions, this was in fact a later development. The earliest pre-conciliar proposal envisioned a document entirely on the Church's relationship to the People of Israel. The draft *Quæstiones de Judaeis* was written by a team of four theologians: Gregory Baum, John Oesterreicher, Leo Rudloff, and George Tavard. Their provocative proposal was presented to the bishops of the Secretariat for Christian Unity in 1961, the year before the Council began. It was rejected, however, because it was felt to be too progressive to send to the Council; the conclusion envisions a reunification of the Church and Synagogue. Tavard challenges us today, forty years after Vatican II, to reconsider this proposal. For this reason, I retrieved the text from the

Msgr. John Oesterreicher archives at Seton Hall University and had it translated for publication here.

Readers will find the overall tone of this book delightfully optimistic. Two senses emerge: one of joyful thanksgiving, and one of hope. The authors acknowledge and celebrate the achievement of *Nostra aetate* in ushering in a new era in relations between Catholics and Jews, and call upon these two faith communities to build on these ties by working in the world more closely and promoting a common moral agenda. As Rabbi Di Segni writes, "We must move forward in ways and with plans yet to be invented for our own good and for the good of everyone." At the same time, the authors express a profound sense of hope that, despite the obstacles of yesterday and the uncertainty of tomorrow, God will continue to guide our two faith communities into God's own future. Let this be our prayer.

In closing, I wish to acknowledge and thank my colleagues who worked for many months to organize the Toronto symposium: Barbara Boraks, Executive Secretary of the Christian-Jewish Dialogue of Toronto; Damian MacPherson, SA, Director of the Commission on Ecumenism and Interreligious Affairs for the Archdiocese of Toronto; John Dadosky, Assistant Professor of Theology at Regis College, Toronto; and Mark Robson, Vice Rector of St. Augustine's Seminary, Toronto.

I am grateful also to a number of other women and men who assisted at various stages in the preparation of this book: Ms. Kathleen S. Dodds, Archival Assistant at Seton Hall University, who scoured the Oesterreicher archives with only fragments of information and provided me with a copy of the schema *Quæstiones de Judaeis*; Dr. Marc B. Cels, for his careful translation of this schema into English; and Prof. Dan Bahat and Ms. Sabrina Berent, for translating Rabbi Di Segni's paper from Italian into English.

Finally, I express my appreciation to Kevin Burns, Commissioning Editor, Novalis, for his insight and advice in preparing the manuscript, and to the editorial team at Novalis for their time and attention to this work. May this book be another sure step forward in the journey of Jews and Catholics together.

Michael Attridge
Toronto, Ontario
October 2006

1

NOSTRA AETATE: FORTY YEARS LATER

George H. Tavard, AA
Professor Emeritus and Theological Adviser to the
Secretariat for Christian Unity
at Vatican II

To look back at *Nostra aetate* is more than a historical exercise, since the genesis of the Second Vatican Council's "Declaration on the Relation of the Church to Non-Christian Religions" (the English title of *Nostra aetate*) has not yet been described in its entirety. Before the story that is generally known, there was a prehistory, when a very elaborate text about Christianity and Judaism was composed during the preparatory phase of the Council in 1961 and 1962. For reasons that I explain, this project never reached the floor of the Council.

The topic is also theological. It hinges on the way the thought of Paul in the Letter to the Romans, chapter 11, has been understood. Most theologians, I believe, have not reflected in depth on the question. Thomas Aquinas is a major exception. Yet his thought, briefly formulated in his commentary on Romans, has had few echoes.[1] As a result, the Pauline insights on Judaism have hardly affected the teaching of the Christian faith in the Catholic Church. If they had, the sufferings of the Jewish people at the hands of Christians could not have taken place to the extent they occurred.

This essay is organized as follows. First, I look briefly at the anti-Judaism of Christians in history. Second, I look at the initiatives of Pope John XXIII. Third, I present the early form of the project *Quæstiones de Judaeis* ("Questions Concerning the Jews"), which was composed in the preparatory period of Vatican Council II, and the difficulties it encountered. Fourth, I look at the subcommission on Judaism that was established in the Vatican's Secretariat for Christian Unity. Fifth, I suggest some reflections on the structure and text of *Nostra aetate*. Finally, I reflect on the background of the document and its follow-up. This leads to a brief conclusion.

---

1   In French: Thomas Aquinas, *Commentaire de l'Epître aux Romains: suivi de Lettre à Bernard Ayglier, abbé du Mont-Cassin* (Paris: Cerf, 1999). There is currently no English translation of this commentary available.

The Anti-Judaism of Christians

Discrimination by Christians against Jews goes back to early patristic times. Justin Martyr's *Dialogue with Trypho* and the *Epistle of Barnabas* contain traces of hostile reaction to the curse on "Christians and heretics" that was formulated in Samuel the Small's treatise *Birkath-ha-Minim*, composed around 85 at Jamnia. Later, in 386/387, eight virulent sermons against Jews were preached in Antioch by John Chrysostom. This anti-Jewish outburst of the future patriarch of Constantinople was occasioned by a Judaizing movement among some Christians who liked to attend the synagogue and celebrate its feasts. It may also have been prompted by a riot, of uncertain date, between Jews and Christians that resulted in an unknown number of victims, presumably on both sides. Despite these few examples, hostility to the Jews remained exceptional among the great Fathers of the Church.

There is little evidence of anti-Judaism in the Carolingian kingdoms, but this sentiment grew and spread in the Middle Ages, notably during the Crusades. Theologians discussed their proper status in Christian kingdoms. Several local councils took protective measures towards Jews, an obvious sign that they needed protection in some places. Popes, however, frequently urged Christian princes to gather and destroy all copies of the Talmud that could be found in their dominions. In 1215, under Innocent III (1198–1216), the

Fourth Lateran Council legislated against Jews and Muslims living in Christian lands. Its Constitutions 67 to 70 decreed the following: The faithful must be protected from the practice of usury by Jews (67); Jews and Muslims must wear distinctive clothing so that they will always be recognizable as not Christian (68); they are forbidden to hold public office (69); and, converts must abandon all Jewish practices (70). When scholastic disputations became fashionable, it was not unusual to force rabbis to take part in disputations with Christian theologians, though this practice had no basis in the Lateran Council.[2] Several kings eventually expelled Jews from their lands, the most notorious being the expulsion from Spain decreed in 1492 by Queen Isabella of Castilla (1451–1504) and her husband Ferdinand of Aragon (1452–1516).

The Renaissance was friendlier to the Jews than the Middle Ages had been. Notable scholars, among them Marsilio Ficino (1433–1499) and Giovanni Pico della Mirandola (1463–1494) in Italy, and Johannes Reuchlin (1455–1522) in Germany, studied the Kabbalah, in which they claimed to find the doctrine of the Trinity.[3] While the Council of Florence did

---

2 The most famous, the disputation of Tortosa, was organized under the authority of Benedict XIII (Pedro de Luna, c.1328, pope in Avignon in 1394, deposed by the Council of Constance in 1417, then residing in Perpignan and finally in Aragon where he was still honoured as pope, d.1423); it lasted about one year and a half, 1413–1414.

3 Avery Dulles, *Princeps Concordiae: Pico della Mirandola and the Scholastic Tradition* (Cambridge, MA: Harvard University Press, 1941).

not pass anti-Jewish regulations, the "Bull of Union with the Copts" (session XI, 4 February 1442) declared that "not only pagans but also Jews or heretics and schismatics, cannot share in eternal life and will go into the everlasting fire which was prepared for the devil and his angels, unless they are joined to the Catholic Church before the end of their lives."[4] By contrast, the "Bull of Union with Syriacs" (session XIII, 30 November 1444) and the "Bull of Union with the Chaldeans and Maronites of Cyprus" (session XIV, 7 August 1445) included no similar statement. I presume that the Copts were thought to be friendly with the Jews. Living in Ethiopia and Egypt, they may have had dealings with the Falasha, the Ethiopian tribe that practises a version of Judaism and claims to descend from the Tribe of Dan.[5]

The Council of Trent did not refer to Jews. Pope Paul IV (1555–1559), however, in his Bull *Cum nimis absurdum* (12 June 1555), decreed measures that were modelled on the Constitutions of the Fourth Lateran Council. The Roman Catechism, published by Pius V (1566–1572) after the Council of Trent, specified that Christians who sin grievously "crucify to themselves again the Son of God," and are more guilty

---

4   Norman Tanner, ed., *Decrees of the Ecumenical Councils*, Vol. 1 (Washington, DC: Georgetown University Press, 1990), 578.

5   The Lemba tribe, which is spread out in South Africa, Zimbabwe, and Tanzania also claims to be one of the lost tribes of Israel. See: Tudor Parfitt, *Journey to the Vanished City: The Search for a Lost Tribe of Israel* (New York: Vintage, 2000).

than Jews.⁶ Logically, this statement implies that Jews as a whole have incurred some degree of guilt for the crucifixion of Jesus.

Shortly before the French Revolution, Henri Grégoire (1750–1831), the pastor in Embermenil, a small village in Lorraine, departed from the general anti-Judaic attitude of Catholic leaders in a paper entitled "Essai sur la régénération physique, morale et politique des juifs,"⁷ which received a prize from the Academy of Metz in 1788. Elected to the Constituent Assembly of the Revolution as a deputy of the clergy, Grégoire initiated the political emancipation of Jews. On 23 December 1789 he presented a motion to grant them full citizenship. Even in this secular political institution he argued on the basis of the Gospel:

> In order to love one's religion it is not necessary to hate or to harass those who are not of it. The one we are happy to profess embraces all people of all countries and all centuries in the bonds of charity; charity is the cry of the Gospel and when I see persecuting

---

6   J. Donovan, trans., *The Catechism of the Council of Trent* (New York: Catholic School Book Co., 1870), 47.

7   Henri Grégoire, *Essai sur la régénération physique, morale et politique des juifs* (Paris: Flammarion, 1988); already in 1785, Grégoire advocated the emancipation of Jews in a sermon preached in Lunéville.

Christians I am tempted to believe that they have not read it.[8]

Grégoire also advanced moral and political arguments. And yet he was by no means an admirer of Judaism. He blamed Jewish isolationism as the main cause of the relegation of Jews to the margins of society. He was convinced, though, of their rights as "men and citizens" in keeping with the general "Declaration of the Rights of Man and of the Citizen" (26 August 1789), and he warmly argued the case for the equality of all humans. The motion he sponsored in favour of Jews was adopted on 27 September 1791 after lengthy debates.[9]

It took a long time for the Church in general to catch up with Grégoire's application of the Gospel to the situation of Jews. The case of the six-year-old child Edgardo Levi Mortara (1852–1940) is well known.[10] Unlike the medieval

---

8   Quoted in Pierre Fauchon, *L'Abbé Grégoire, le prêtre-citoyen* (Tours: Editions de la Nouvelle-République, 1989), 30.

9   In October 1789, Grégoire also composed a *Mémoire en faveur des gens de couleur ou sangs mêlés de Saint Domingue et des autres îles françaises de l'Amérique*. About the same time he joined the *Société des amis des noirs*. He was instrumental in the abolition of slavery: on 27 July 1793 the Convention outlawed all subsidies for the slave trade; on 4 February 1794 it abolished slavery in the French colonies.

10 On 23/24 June 1858, the child was removed from his parents' care by the police of the Papal States on orders from the Roman Inquisition because a maid declared that she had baptized him while he was sick. Taken to Rome, he was raised as a ward of Pius IX. In standard Catholic theology the natural law is more binding than the positive law of State or Church. Yet in this case the Pope put aside the parents' natural rights and

collections of canons, however, the code of 1917 prepared under Leo XIII (1878–1903) and Pius X (1903–1914) and published by Benedict XV (1914–1922) mentioned neither Jews nor Israel nor the Talmud. Conferences with Jews on religious matters were covered by the general regulation of canon 1325 §3: Authorization is required, in general from the Holy See, or in urgent cases from the Ordinary, to hold "debates or conferences" with all who are not Catholic.[11] Meanwhile, in 1928 the Holy Office in Rome declared that the Church condemns (*damnat*) any kind of hatred against the Jewish people. In his encyclical *Mit brennender sorge* (14 March 1937), Pius XI condemned the anti-Semitism of the National Socialists in Germany.

---

duties in order to protect the integrity of an alleged baptism by a maid. I say "alleged" because the maid's description of what she did should have raised a doubt about her performance of the rite: She apparently threw a few drops of water on the baby's head before saying the Trinitarian formula, whereas the words should accompany the pouring of water. When he was sixteen, Mortara paid a visit to his parents but decided not to live with them. He became an Augustinian canon and was ordained in 1873. This, however, does not excuse the policy of Pius IX, who was directly involved in the incident. See David Kertzer, *The Kidnapping of Edgardo Mortara* (New York: Alfred Knopf, 1997).

11 "Let Catholics beware lest they have debates or conferences, especially public ones, with non-Catholics without having come to the Holy See or, if the case is urgent, to the local Ordinary." See Edward N. Peters, curator, *The 1917 or Pio-Benedictine Code of Canon Law: In English Translation with Extensive Scholarly Apparatus* (San Francisco: Ignatius Press, 2001).

The Initiatives of John XXIII

Angelo Roncalli (1881–1963) was apostolic nuncio to Turkey and Bulgaria from 1925 to 1937, and to Greece from 1938 to December 1944, when he became apostolic nuncio in Paris. During World War II, he worked tirelessly to save Jews from Hitler's persecution. He managed to provide thousands of them in Bulgaria and Hungary with false baptismal certificates and even false travelling visas, thanks to which many escaped arrest and were able to leave occupied Europe and reach Palestine. He was elected bishop of Rome on 28 October 1958, taking the name of John XXIII. In 1959, he altered the liturgy of Good Friday, replacing a prayer *pro perfidis Judaeis* with a prayer *pro Judaeis*. In context, the Latin word *perfidus* did not mean "perfidious" but "unbelieving." Vernacular translations, however, tended to suggest "perfidy." Some time later, as his car passed the great Synagogue of Rome, Pope John stopped and spontaneously gave a blessing to the people who had just come out and were gathered in front of the building.

Pope John XXIII surprised everyone in January 1960 when he announced that he would call a general council. In the remote preparation of the Council he asked bishops, Catholic universities, and the Roman dicasteries for advice concerning the conciliar agenda. In a letter dated 26 April 1960, the University of Fribourg in Switzerland recommended condemning the anti-Semitism of Christians. The university declared three propositions unacceptable: first, "the Jews rejected and crucified Jesus"; second, "the believers from the Gentiles have been elected instead of the people of Israel"; and third, "the People of Israel have been rejected by God for ever." In addition, the university recommended that Christians should pray "that the prophecy in Rom 11:25-26 be fulfilled and the People of Israel be placed in the elect locus reserved for it in the Church of Christ."[12]

In the preparatory period of the Council, Pope John instructed the German Cardinal Augustine Bea to prepare a conciliar statement about Judaism. Bea in turn entrusted the work to Msgr. John Oesterreicher. Born into a Jewish family in the Austrian Empire, Oesterreicher (1904–1993) was baptized in 1924 and ordained in 1928. In 1943 he founded the Institute of Judeo-Christian Studies at Seton Hall University in the United States.

The First Project

Oesterreicher asked a few members and consultants of the Secretariat for Christian Unity to form a small group of advisers. This group included Abbot Leo Rudloff of the Dormition Abbey in Jerusalem and Weston Priory in Vermont; Gregory Baum, then a professor at the University of St.

---

12 *Acta et documenta concilio œcumenico vaticano II apparando*. Series I, Vol. IV, Pars II. (Vatican City: Typis polyglottis vaticanis, 1961), 784–786.

Michael's College in Toronto; and me, at the time the chair of the theology department at Mount Mercy College, now Carlow University, in Pittsburgh, PA. This unofficial "North American team" met several times in New Jersey and composed a draft document in 1961.[13]

The draft, entitled *Quæstiones de Judaeis*, was presented to a plenary meeting of the Secretariat for Christian Unity in August 1961 at Roca di Papa, near Rome. This first draft followed this outline:

Part One: Principia dogmatica

1. De ecclesiæ radicibus in Vetere Testamento
2. De Iudæis perpetuo dilectis a Deo
3. De ultima reconciliatione Synagogæ cum Ecclesia

Part Two: Considerationes morales et liturgicæ

4. De Iudæis fratribus nostris separatis
5. De festis virorum iustorum Veteris Testamenti

Part Three: Observationes practicæ

6. De instructione seminaristarum et catechistarum
7. De continuatione operis dilectionis a Summo Pontifice instituti
8. De ecclesiae præsentia in Terra Sancta[14]

---

13 On this "North American team," however, was Oesterreicher from Austria, Rudloff and Baum from Germany, and me from France!

14 Part One: Dogmatic Principles
1. The Roots of the Church in the Old Testament

Each section ended with a recommendation that summed it up. The first section was theological, and proposed an interpretation of Paul's teaching in Romans 11 on the eventual reunion of the Synagogue and the Church. The second was liturgical, and intended to familiarize the non-theological laity with the doctrinal status of Judaism, to promote feelings of brotherhood between Catholics and Jews, and to insert the hope of reconciliation in the prayer life of the faithful. The third was practical, and aimed at reshaping the formation of seminarians and catechists in order to improve the Church's contribution to reconciliation with Jews. Since the text dealt with the presence of the Church in the Holy Land, it implicitly recognized the lasting value of the State of Israel. When this text was presented to the plenary gathering of the Secretariat for Christian Unity on 26–31 August 1961 at Roca di Papa, it provoked a high degree of astonishment among several of the bishops who were members of the Secretariat. The ensuing

---

2. The Jews are Forever Loved by God
3. The Ultimate Reconciliation of the Synagogue with the Church
Part Two: Moral and Liturgical Considerations
4. The Jews are Our Separated Brethren
5. Feasts of the Righteous Men of the Old Testament
Part Three: Practical Observations
6. Instructions to Seminarians and Catechists
7. Continuation of the Loving Work Instituted by the Most High Pontiff
8. The Presence of the Church in the Holy Land

discussion showed that there was also a certain amount of disagreement.

In the following months, the North American group attempted to safeguard the heart of its project. We shortened the text, brought it from thirteen to six pages, and reduced the recommendations from eight to four. The references to Romans 9–11 were reduced to a general mention in the introduction, with the affirmation that God's gifts and call are without repentance (Rom 11:29). We omitted several things: the proposal for a feast of the Just of the Old Testament, several practical observations and recommendations (including the neuralgic question of the formation of seminarians), and all allusions to the State of Israel. The result was presented again to the Secretariat in November in Bühl, Germany. The full text of this second draft, which had the following outline, appears in English translation in the appendix to this book.

Introduction: Quoting the Apostle Paul and Thomas Aquinas

1. The Roots of the Church in the Old Testament. Argumentation from Augustine and from the Paschal liturgy. The Church is a living continuation of the People of Israel. There is only one economy of salvation. It includes the Old Testament and the New Testament.

2. The Jews are Still Beloved of God. Quote from Cardinal Achille Liénart.

3. The Final Reconciliation of the Synagogue with the Church is Part of the Christian Hope, though its Modality Remains a Mystery. References to Theodore of Mopsuestia, Gregory the Great, Photius of Constantinople, and Origen.

4. Jews Are Our Separated Brothers. Citation of Pius XI: "Spiritually, we are Semites"; Reference to John XXIII. Condemnation of racism and antisemitism (the term "deicide" was not used).

In spite of this redraft of our previous dogmatic, liturgical, and practical considerations, the project was discarded in its entirety in June 1962 at the next plenary meeting of the Secretariat.[15] Given the difficulties raised within the Secretariat, though not by its officials, it was fairly certain that the text as we had conceived it would not obtain the necessary conciliar majority of two thirds of the votes. It was clear that, in order to be accepted by the Council, the statement on Judaism had to meet a number of political and practical conditions. The North American group had systematically focused attention on doctrine and the interpretation of the relevant passages in Paul's Letter to the Romans. Largely because of the former Abbot of the Dormition's influence,

---

15 Claude Soetens, "The Ecumenical Commitment of the Catholic Church," in *History of Vatican II*, Vol. III, eds. Giuseppe Alberigo and Joseph A. Komonchack (Maryknoll, NY: Orbis, 2000), 276.

it also had seen the emergence of the State of Israel as a providential event that was likely to renovate modern Judaism and thus to present the Church with an extraordinary occasion to review and renew its own stance in regard to the Jews. We had not said this officially, though, because of the political situation in Palestine and the fact that the Holy See did not officially recognize the State of Israel. Yet it clearly stood in the background of the text.

Most bishops at Vatican II were certainly not opposed to theological speculation on the religious status of Judaism. However, many of them lived in countries where there were no or only a few Jews and did not feel any urgency to upgrade Christian-Jewish relations. Outside of Europe, few were haunted by memories of the Shoah and by the question whether Pius XII should have done more to thwart Hitler's plan of genocide. Yet the question could not be ignored because it was dramatically posed in Germany, precisely in 1963, by Rolf Hochhuth's play *Der Stellvertreter* (The Deputy).

Generally, the bishops did not wish to choose among possible theological interpretations of the thought of the Apostle Paul. Above all, they had a double pastoral concern: first, about life in pluralistic societies in which the State protects religious freedom; and second, about the conditions under which Christians live in Muslim societies where the dominant Islamic culture is commonly favoured by the government. It was understandable that bishops in those areas felt a primary interest in relations with Islam. Some of them anticipated heavy criticism if they returned home with a declaration that sounded favourable to Jews in the Israel-Arab conflict. It was particularly striking that all the Patriarchs of Eastern Catholic Churches and all the bishops of the Melkite Church considered any statement inopportune if it could be read as favouring Jews over Arabs in the Near East. It was largely because of this opposition that when a totally new draft was distributed on 8 November 1963, the Secretariat for Christian Unity issued a statement to the effect that "the document is entirely religious in its contents and spiritual in its purpose."[16]

The New Subcommission

Given these conditions, a larger subcommission in the Secretariat for Christian Unity was charged with composing a new draft. Thomas Holland, auxiliary bishop of Portsmouth, chaired this subcommission. Barnabas Ahern, CP, Gregory Baum, OSA, and Msgr. John Oesterreicher were the members, and Thomas Stransky, CSP, was the secretary. Two specialists, Bruno Hussar, OP, from Israel, and Msgr. A. C. Ramselaar from the Netherlands, were also brought in. Other experts were

---

16 Xavier Rynne, *The Second Session: The Debates and Decrees of Vatican Council II, September 29 to December 4, 1963* (New York: Farrar, Straus and Company), 364–365.

called in later to help with the treatment of other religions. In substance, this group wrote the text that would become Article 4 of the final draft of *Nostra aetate*.

The new draft passed through several stages. The question of where to place the text within the conciliar documents emerged early: Should the statement on Judaism be a chapter in the Decree on Ecumenism, or an appendix to it? Should it be included in the Constitution on the Church? Should it be placed in what was then Schema XIII (the document that would become the Pastoral Constitution on the Church in the Modern World)? On 9 October 1964, Cardinal Bea spoke to the Secretariat for Christian Unity, reading a letter from Paul VI. The Pope recommended creating a mixed commission that would include a statement on Judaism in the Constitution on the Church. This idea, however, was not pursued because of numerous objections. In fact, the text on Judaism had become Chapter Four in the Decree on Ecumenism the year before, when Cardinal Bea introduced it to the Council on 18 November 1963. At the beginning of the third session it was presented as an appendix to the ecumenism text. Finally, largely on a recommendation made by Cardinal Carlo Confalonieri (1893–1986) of the Conciliar Coordinating Commission on 16–17 April 1964, it became a separate document, but downgraded to the rank of "declaration." While much talk went back and forth on points of where to locate the document and what it would be called, I never doubted that the logic of the topic required the document to be self-standing, whatever it was called.

As Cardinal Bea introduced the successive forms of the text on Judaism to the Council, he spoke strongly in favour of a forceful statement. He argued in part from fundamental principles regarding the roots of Christianity in the Jewish people and in part from the horrors of the Shoah and from the moral duty to fight anti-Semitism. It soon appeared that there was uncertainty among the bishops whether the word "deicide," which the text considered inappropriate in Christian references to Jews, should be mentioned at all. The North American group had not used it. The drafters who inserted it aimed at putting a definitive end to the non-theological language of some Christians who designated the Jewish people, collectively, as deicide – or, in more vulgar English parlance, as "God-killers" or "Christ-killers." An explicit ban on this accusation was strongly supported by several American bishops. One could infer from the evidence of the New Testament that the Jews who opposed Jesus did not believe that he was the Christ and that they could have no awareness of his divinity. Moreover, the term was generally distasteful and insulting to contemporary Jews, who cannot be responsible for what some Jews did almost 2,000 years ago. Others, meanwhile, feared that if the term was omitted it could give rise to a misunderstanding that the crucified Jesus was no longer seen as the Second Person of the Holy Trinity, divine in the true sense of the term, even while incarnate.

In 1964, at the beginning of the third session, the word "deicide" had been removed and the reference to persecutions of Jews by Christians had been toned down. The Latin word *vexatio* (harassment) replaced the stronger term *persecutio* (persecution), even though it sounds rather weak in vernacular translations. Among others, two American cardinals, Richard Cushing of Boston and Joseph Ritter of St. Louis, strongly supported the text. Of those who openly wanted to speak favourably of the Jews, Bishop Fulton Sheen stands out. In a written intervention dated 27 February 1964, he justified such a stance by referring to Romans 11, with this curious reason: "Not only are the Jews our fathers, they also will be our future descendents."[17] He had therefore made their future conversion the main reason for contemporary friendship. In any case, whatever his theological motivation, his openness towards Jews is all the more to be noticed as Sheen was reticent in regard to an ecumenical recognition of baptisms administered by Protestant ministers.[18]

---

17 "*Judæi non solum patres nostri ferunt, sed etiam nostra futura progenies erunt.*" In *Acta et documenta concilio œcumenico vaticano II apparando*. Series I, Vol. III, Pars VI. (Vatican City: Typis polyglottis vaticanis, 1961), 498; see also the written intervention on *"Habitudo catholicorum ad Judæos,"* dated 27 Februrary 1964, in *Acta synodalia sacrosancti concilii œcumenici vaticani II*. Appendix I. (Vatican City: Typis polyglottis vaticanis, 1983), 498–500.

18 The reason, he alleged, was a widespread denial of original sin; Sheen recommended placing the authority to recognize the validity of such baptisms in the hands of apostolic nuncios.

The turning point in the composition of *Nostra aetate* came when, in view of the oriental Patriarchs' continued objections, several bishops suggested that the Council should speak not only of Judaism but also of Islam. Muslims, too, they argued, believe in the God of Abraham, and the Quran identifies Jesus and Mary as authentic prophets of God. This discussion ended on 29 September 1964; the Secretariat for Christian Unity then started to work to expand the proposed draft. Experts were brought in to help write new paragraphs. Nearly two months later, on 20 November, Cardinal Bea presented the resulting version, which now spoke also of three great religions: Hinduism, Buddhism, and Islam. This text was accepted in substance on 21 November 1964, with 1651 votes in favour, 242 in favour with modifications, 99 against, and 4 votes that were invalid.

During the fourth session of the Council, on 14 October 1965, Cardinal Bea gave his last presentation of the schema in its final form. A vote on 15 October showed 1763 in favour, 1 in favour with modifications, 250 against, and 9 invalid. The final vote on 28 October carried a much higher majority: 2221 in favour, 2 in favour with modifications, 88 against, and 1 invalid. The lines relating to the Hindu, Buddhist, and Islamic religions had rallied most of the opponents. *Nostra aetate* was promulgated on the same day. In his address, Paul VI said that the document refers "above all to the Hebrews, of whom it speaks so that they be neither rejected nor subject to mistrust, but rather that respect and love be shown to them and hope placed in them."[19] In this subtle sentence Pope Paul specified respect, love, and hope as the proper Christian attitude towards Jews, but avoided committing himself to a specific description of this hope.

Nostra aetate

The structure of the "Declaration on the Relation of the Church to Non-Christian Religions" is as follows:

- **Article 1** is on the existence of the religions and the unity of the human race. *Nostra aetate* begins with a consideration of the general religiosity that is attested to by the universal fact of the existence of religions.
- **Article 2** briefly describes the two great religions of Asia: Hinduism and Buddhism. The faithful are exhorted to know, assist, and promote the spiritual and moral goods and the socio-cultural values of these religions.
- **Article 3** acknowledges and describes Islam.
- In **Article 4**, consideration of Judaism is reduced to the following points:

---

19 "...*maxime Hebraei, quibuscum sic agitur ut non reprobentur neque iis diffidatur, sed ut erga eos reverentia et amor adhibeatur spesque in iis collocetur.*"

- The spiritual union of Christians with the descendents of Abraham
- The status of Christians as "children of Abraham according to the faith"
- The origin of Christianity in the Old Testament
- The birth of Jesus from his Jewish mother, Mary, and the first evangelization done chiefly by Jewish Christians
- The permanence of God's Covenant
- The common spiritual patrimony of Jews and Christians
- The willing death of Christ for all humans because of the sins of all, and the Gospel of the cross of Christ as the sign of God's love and the source of grace

- **Article 5** condemns anti-Semitism, racism, and discrimination based on religion. The conclusion returns to the theme of religious peace and fraternity, and reproves all discrimination against members of non-Christian religions. All are urged to forget their past conflicts, to strive for mutual understanding and for the promotion of justice, morality, peace, and liberty. In all the documents issued from the Second Vatican Council, this comes closest to a list of anathemas.

Reflections

It is clear that a double movement presided over the drafting. On the one hand, the original idea of a statement limited to Judaism was replaced by the broader ambition of addressing most of the major religions. On the other hand, the Declaration never intended to be an exercise in comparative religion. And though the Fathers of the Church saw intimations of Christianity in the pagan myths of their time, there was no attempt to make similar suggestions concerning the great religions of the modern world.

Due to the existing tension between the State of Israel and its Muslim neighbours, the non-political nature of the Declaration needed to be unquestionable. This non-political character would have been more immediately evident if the relevant passage had been cast as a reflection on monotheism in its various contemporary forms, including the old religion of Zoroaster, Sikhism, and the more recent Baha'i movement. No one at the time suggested it. Yet it could have elegantly cushioned the lines on Islam, which were composed by a Dominican scholar from Egypt, Georges Chehata Anawati (1905–1994), who was eager to use formulas that could evoke the language of the Quran when translated into Arabic.

If a few lines about Islam were likely to placate the bishops of Muslim areas and gain their support for the Declaration, the proper balance of the document required analogous attention to be paid to the great religions of Asia. Sympathetic allusions to Hinduism and Buddhism would please the people of continental Asia and Japan and encourage the bishops to maintain or develop positive relations with the traditional religions of their lands. A number of bishops were acquainted with the attempts of Yves Monchanin (1895–1957), Henri Le Saux (1910–1973), and Bede Griffiths (1906–1994) to adapt Christian monachism to the monastic traditions of India. And most were willing to encourage what was at the same time an inculturation of Catholic spirituality and a possible enrichment of it by Hindu or Buddhist spiritualism. While it avoided references to their mythologies, the text focused attention on the spiritual horizon of the beliefs and practices of these great religions.

Although it was considerably shorter than the original North American project, the treatment of Judaism had to remain longer than that of any other particular religion. The Church had to acknowledge the historic and doctrinal origin of the Christian faith in the Old Testament and in the Judaism of Jesus' time along with the Jewishness of Jesus and his Mother, of the Apostles, and of the first generations of Christian believers. An extensive consideration of Judaism, however, could have been seen as improper in the eyes of the other world religions. The text therefore had to be carefully balanced while remaining succinct.

The setting of the reflections on Judaism in the fundamental religious orientation of humankind and alongside the major religions of the world could convey the impression that in the eyes of the Catholic Church, Judaism counts as just one religion among others. This very question was explicitly debated in the Secretariat for Christian Unity. If one holds that the Covenant with Moses was abolished with the death and resurrection of Jesus, then the status of the continuing Judaism after the destruction of the Temple becomes problematic. The idea that Judaism after the beginning of Christianity lost its privileged standing and therefore should be a target of the Christian mission just like any other religion was defended in the Secretariat for Christian Unity by the Dutch theologian Franz Thijssen. His view, however, was not shared by most in the Secretariat. Retained from the earliest draft, but rewritten and reorganized, were the sections on the ties of Christianity with the Old Testament and the Judaism of Jesus' time, on God's continuing love and Covenant with Israel, and on the condemnation of anti-Semitism.

The tone of the Declaration turned out to be quite different from that of the original project. The accent is primarily on the mystery of the Church rather than on God's Covenant with Israel. The Church's hope for the reconciliation of Judaism is still present, but it is conceived as an eventual, presumably remote acceptance of Jesus as the Messiah by Jews, not as a reconciliation of the Church with the Synagogue. In other words, the Declaration remains within the general framework of the usual theological reflection on Judaism. Unlike the North American project, it does not depart essentially from what has been a fundamental Catholic stance through the centuries, even though it is much more open – not only to peaceful coexistence between Christians and Jews, but also to a fraternal dialogue between them regarding the problems of contemporary society. I see the heart of the Declaration in the following statement:

> The Church cannot forget that she received the revelation of the Old Covenant through that people with which God in his infinite mercy deigned to initiate the Old Covenant, and that she was fed from the root of the good olive tree into which the wild olive branches of the Gentiles have been grafted. The Church believes that Christ, our Peace, reconciled Jews and Gentiles through the Cross and made both of them one in Himself. (Article 4)

After evoking the ignorance of the Gospel by most of Jesus' contemporaries and the active opposition of "not a few" to the spread of the Gospel, the Declaration maintains that Jews remain beloved of God, both because God's "gifts and callings are without repentance," and "on account of their fathers." The Council declares that, like the Prophets and the Apostle Paul, the Church "waits for the day, known to God alone, when all peoples will praise the Lord with one voice ...." The consequence follows that although the "Jewish authorities" planned "the death of Christ, neither all the Jews of the time nor those of today can be blamed for the Passion." Therefore, while the Church is "the new people of God, the Jews are neither reprobate nor cursed by God" (Article 4).

Because there had been extensive debates about possible implications of the word "deicide," the term was omitted. The Declaration is also silent on what has been constitutive of Jewish life and worship since the destruction of the Second Temple. Neither the teachings of the Talmud nor the religious function of the Synagogue nor the mystical doctrines of the Kabbalah are mentioned. In fact, they were never debated. No negative judgment is passed on contemporary Judaism. It is unfortunate, however, that while the value of Hinduism, Buddhism, and Islam is located in these religions as they stand today, the value of the Jewish religion is seen only in relation to the Old Covenant. Unlike the discarded early draft, the Declaration, as it expresses the hope that Jews will eventually recognize Jesus as the Messiah, does not look forward to a reconciliation of the Synagogue and the Church. The perspective of reconciliation does not evoke *vitam ex mortuis*, "life from the dead" (Rom 11:15). It is not seen as a resurrection, a new flowering of faith and life for all Christians.

The Declaration affirms that God's Covenant with Israel persists. Yet it does not explain what the substance of this Covenant can be for those who do not recognize that, in

Christian terms, the Messiah has come. The Church indeed must "announce the cross of Christ as the sign of God's universal love and the source [*fontem*] of all grace." This sign, however, is valid for the whole world, and no special relevance to Jews is suggested.

Pope Paul's Journeys

An interesting background to the debates on *Nostra aetate* is provided by the amount of travelling that took place, more or less, in relation to the Declaration. In his address at the closing of the second session on 4 December 1963, Pope Paul expressed his intention to go on pilgrimage to the land of Jesus. He travelled there on 4 January 1964 and returned two days later. This was a bold initiative, since the Holy See did not officially recognize the State of Israel. The Pope landed in Jordan and was escorted into Israel by a Jordanian police escort. Theologically, the visit was not planned as an encounter with Judaism but with the Orthodox. The Bishop of Rome had his historic meeting with the Ecumenical Patriarch Athenagoras (1886–1972, patriarch in 1948). As they prayed the Lord's Prayer together, they shattered the traditional ban on *communicatio in divinis* ("communication on holy matters"). Paul VI also met with the Greek Patriarch of Jerusalem, Benedictos I (patriarch, 1957–1980), and with the Armenian Patriarch of St. James, Yeghishe Derderian (patriarch, 1960–1990).

During the third session of the Council, Pope Paul travelled once again. In New York City on 4 October 1964 he addressed the General Assembly of the United Nations. Next, he flew to Bombay to attend a Eucharistic Congress from 2–5 December 1964. On the way to India he stopped at the Beirut airport for a few hours and met with the president of Lebanon. Pope Paul also used the occasion of his presence in India to address the members of the non-Christian religions. He even quoted from the Brihadaranyaka Upanishad: "From the unreal lead me to the real; from darkness lead me to light; from death lead me to immortality" (Brih. 1, 3, 28). This must have been the first time that an Upanishad was cited in a pontifical document. After this journey, on 9 December 1964, Pope Paul addressed a friendly letter to the Catholic and Orthodox Patriarchs living in Arabic countries.[20] These travels helped to shape the context of catholicity in which the Declaration makes sense.

Cardinal Bea also did some travelling, which was directly connected with the conciliar debates. At the end of March and beginning of April 1963, he visited New York City and Boston, where he presented several essays. During this time he met with bishops and officials of the American Jewish Committee, most notably with Rabbi Abraham Heschel (1907–1972).

---

20 "Lettre de S.S. Paul VI aux patriarches catholiques et orthodoxes des pays arabes," *La Documentation Catholique* 1440 (17 January 1965): cols. 143–146.

The strong opposition of the Eastern Catholic Churches and a few hostile statements made by Orthodox hierarchs suggested that political tensions might cause the Declaration to be misunderstood and possibly misused. Therefore, after a plenary meeting of the Secretariat for Christian Unity that took place on 3–4 March 1965, the secretary, Msgr. Jan Willebrands, and an Arabic-speaking staff member, Pierre Duprey, MAfr, travelled to the Near East and met with Eastern Catholic prelates. Again, because of demonstrations in the streets of Damascus and other cities against the proposed Declaration, another delegation, comprised of Willebrands, the Belgian Bishop Emiel-Jozef De Smedt (one of the chief writers of the Declaration on Religious Freedom), and Duprey, travelled again to the Near East to visit the Eastern Catholic and several Orthodox patriarchs.

It will come as no surprise that the bishops of the United States were highly supportive of the statement on Judaism. On 28 September 1964, Cardinals Richard Cushing (1895–1970) of Boston, Albert Meyer (1903–1965) of Chicago, and Joseph Ritter (1892–1967) of St. Louis spoke in favour of it. On 29 September, Stephen Leven (1905–1983), auxiliary bishop of San Antonio, and Patrick O'Boyle (1896–1987), archbishop of Washington, followed along the same lines. In 1965, before the Fourth Session of the Council, the American bishops created a commission of ten members headed by Francis Leipzig (1895–1981), bishop of Baker, Oregon. To this commission, they entrusted the task of contacting representative organs of the American Jewish community and supervising Jewish-Catholic dialogues in the US.

After the Council, when it was time to begin the implementation of the conciliar decisions, the wide scope of *Nostra aetate* was divided among subcommissions. Article 4 remained the responsibility of the President of the Secretariat for Christian Unity and of the Secretariat itself, functioning as a Commission for Religious Relations with Jews. In January 1975 this commission issued "Guidelines and Suggestions for Implementing the Conciliar Declaration *Nostra aetate* (No. 4)." Meanwhile, on Pentecost Sunday 1964, Paul VI created the Secretariat for Non-Christians (responsible for Articles 2 and 3 of the Declaration) and the Secretariat for Dialogue with Non-Believers. These commissions were upgraded by Pope John Paul II, who named them "councils" in 1988. The Secretariat for Non-Christians became the Pontifical Council for Inter-Religious Dialogue. In 1982, John Paul II created a Pontifical Council for Culture, with which he amalgamated the Secretariat for Dialogue with Non-Believers on 25 March 1993.

Conclusion

On the whole, the debates about Judaism in the Secretariat for Christian Unity and in the Second Vatican Council revealed that the Catholic hierarchy in general was very much in favour of better relations between Jews and Christians. The difference between the early North American project and the final product, however, suggests that the hierarchy was not prepared to envisage the advisability, or the possibility, of an approach to contemporary Judaism that would place it within the scope of the ecumenical commitment of the Catholic Church in regards to Christian communities. Advisability is mostly a matter of politics and diplomacy. Possibility is a question of theology. It was not clear at the time, nor is it clear today, whether our diverging allegiances to the Bible offer a sufficient foundation for the fraternity of Jews and Christians that was envisaged in the early draft of *Quæstiones de Judaeis*. This lack of clarity hinges on two points. First, in spite of Jerome's advocacy of *hebraica veritas*, the Catholic reading of the Bible has traditionally favoured the Septuagint over the Hebrew Bible, for the obvious reason that Greek soon replaced Aramaic as the dominant language of the early Church. Second, the Christian reading has generally ignored the data of the Talmud, which should be read as a history of Jewish interpretations, a history in which anecdotes, back-and-forth arguments, and personal idiosyncrasies can be just as meaningful as the overall picture.

In the Decree on Ecumenism, the bishops accepted the nature and conditions of inter-Christian ecumenical relationships based on the commonality of the New Testament.

The basis for a similar relationship with Judaism is implicit in the Jewish origin of the Christian faith, in the meditation on the Temple and the Tabernacle that runs through the Letter to the Hebrews, and in Paul's reflections in the Letter to the Romans on the Judaism of his time and of times to come. Nevertheless, following the synod of Jamnia (whether this was an actual gathering makes little difference), the separation of two biblical traditions, the excommunication of Jewish Christians from the Synagogue, and the ensuing hostility of the two groups make a fully ecumenical relation of Christians and Jews somewhat utopian, although not unthinkable.

Ecumenism is not a one-way street. It has to grow together with the partners in dialogue. It presupposes an antecedent willingness to walk together, to think together, and to venture together in new ways. Should the desire for fellowship increase, the modalities of a new relationship of Christians and Jews will have to be determined together. It is time for rabbis and Christian theologians to reflect jointly on what their relationships could become if they were eager to welcome one another, as the Decree on Ecumenism puts it, *par cum pari* ("in total parity"). That the Council did not urge such a course of action is not surprising. The task of a Council is not to open new chapters in theology. The North American draft dared to propose a prophetic vision, knowing full well that the proposal would cause concern and hesitancies and that its implementation, if accepted, would take a long time.

The horizon envisaged was not negated by the Council, since the Council as such never saw the text. It was the prudence of the Secretariat for Christian Unity that chose not to present it, for fear it could not gather the majority required for endorsement.

This history can be interpreted in two ways. It can mean that the North American proposal was intrinsically inappropriate and therefore unacceptable. It can also mean that the Catholic hierarchy was not ready for such a departure from past views of Judaism by Christians. In my opinion, the latter was precisely the case. And one may wonder if the situation has become significantly better. Who among Catholic bishops and theologians is looking forward, with Photius of Constantinople, to the reconciliation of Jews and Christians as to an occasion of "perfect and universal joy"?[21] Perhaps Photius is too Greek. But the testimony of Thomas Aquinas cannot be easily pushed aside. As he read Paul's question and answer – "For if their rejection is the reconciliation of the world, what will their acceptance be but life from the dead!" (Rom 11:15) – Aquinas understood that "The re-assumption of Jews by God will make the Gentiles resurrect into life."[22] He wondered who the Gentiles were

---

21 Karl Staab, *Pauluskommentare: aus der griechischen Kirche aus Katenenhandschriften* (Münster: Aschendorff, 1933), 526.

22 Thomas Aquinas, "Commentary on the Letter to the Romans," caput XI, lectio II, ad 11,15 in *Opera Omnia* Vol. XX, (Paris: Vivès, 1876), 539.

who were in need of resurrection. He suggested that they might be Christians with lukewarm faith or Christians misled by the Antichrist. He also suggested that the "conversion of Jews" might be an eschatological event immediately prior to the general resurrection of the flesh. In fact, I was taught this last view in the catechism of my childhood. These tentative interpretations evidently show that Aquinas was not certain of Paul's meaning. His hesitancy, however, does not tone down his forceful conclusion: "Ignorance of this mystery would be damning for us."[23]

---

23 *Sed ignorantia hujus mysterii esset nobis damnosa*, in Thomas Aquinas, "Commentary on the Letter to the Romans," caput XI, lectio IV, ad 11,25 in *Opera Omnia* Vol. XX, (Paris: Vivès, 1876), 542.

2

JEWISH-CATHOLIC RELATIONS FROM *NOSTRA AETATE* TO THE PRESENT

Ovey N. Mohammed, SJ
Professor Emeritus, Regis College,
University of Toronto

The literature on Jewish-Catholic relations for the last forty years is extensive. For this reason, I will limit myself to an examination of five magisterial documents:

i) "Declaration on the Relation of the Church to Non-Christian Religions" [*Nostra aetate*], issued by the Second Vatican Council on 28 October 1965;

ii) "Guidelines and Suggestions for Implementing the Conciliar Declaration *Nostra aetate* Article 4" [*Guidelines*], issued by the Vatican Commission for Religious Relations with the Jews on 21 December 1974;

iii) "Notes on the Correct Way to Present the Jews and Judaism in Preaching and Catechesis in the Roman Catholic Church" [*Notes*], issued by the Vatican Commission for Religious Relations with the Jews on 24 June 1985;

iv) "We Remember: A Reflection on the Shoah" [*We Remember*], issued by the same Commission on 17 March 1998; and

v) "*Dominus Iesus*: On the Unicity and Salvific Universality of Jesus Christ and the Church" [*Dominus Iesus*], issued by the Vatican's Congregation for the Doctrine of the Faith on 6 August 2000.

Nostra aetate

To better appreciate the significance of *Nostra aetate*, it is helpful to recall briefly some of the anti-Jewish polemic in the Christian tradition. The New Testament itself contains these claims: that the Covenant God made with Christians replaced the Covenant God made with the Jews; that typological readings of the Old Testament reveal that the prophets predicted the coming of Christ; that Jews were responsible for the death of Jesus; that the Jews are cursed and children of the devil; and that the Pharisees were hypocrites who hated Jesus. In the patristic period, these anti-Jewish motifs passed into the thinking of the Church Fathers. They in turn developed an anti-Jewish theology in which the Jews were doomed to wander the earth to the end of time for their iniquity and faithlessness to God and as living proof of the truth of the Christian faith.

With the passing of the patristic period, the basic pattern of Christian theological anti-Judaism had been established. It was not until the twentieth century that this comprehensive anti-Jewish thinking saw the beginning of a reversal in Christian consciousness. There can be little doubt that three events played a major role in setting the stage for this reversal: i) the systematic torture and genocide of six million Jews in countries long considered Christian, a point acknowledged in the *Guidelines* (p. 31)[1]; ii) the founding of the State of Israel in 1948, which defied Christian ideas of the wandering Jew; and iii) the advent of biblical criticism, which relativized the authority of scriptural polemics, making it no longer acceptable to absolutize New Testament debates into eternal anti-Jewish principles.

When the Second Vatican Council issued *Nostra aetate*,[2] it began by dissociating itself from the claim that Christianity has displaced Judaism in God's plan of salvation. Instead, it

---

[1] The page numbers refer to the text of the *Guidelines* as found in Eugene J. Fisher and Leon Klenicki, eds., *In Our Time: The Flowering of the Jewish-Catholic Dialogue* (New York: Paulist Press, 1990), 29–37.

[2] The page numbers refer to the text of *Nostra aetate* as found in Fisher and Klenicki, *In Our Time*, 27–28.

speaks of the "spiritual bond" linking Jews and Christians (p. 27) and of the "spiritual patrimony" common to both (p. 28), and officially admits to the Jewish roots of Christianity: "The Church of Christ acknowledges that, according to the mystery of God's saving design, the beginnings of its faith and its election are already found among the patriarchs, Moses and the Prophets" (p. 27). Using the vibrant imagery of root and branch in Paul's Letter to the Romans (p. 27), the document acknowledges in the present tense that the Church cannot "forget that it draws sustenance from the root of that good olive tree onto which have been grafted the wild olive branches of the Gentiles" (cf. Rom 11:17-24).

Nostra aetate then cites a key passage from Romans 9:4-5 in which Paul speaks of the Jewish people, even after the coming of Christ, as those "who have the adoption of sons, and the glory and the Covenant, and the legislation and the worship and the promise" (p. 27). The present tense in these citations is a clear admission that the Jews remain in relationship with God, that they worship God legitimately, and that their continued observance of the Torah is a sign of their ongoing fidelity to God. As Paul knew, and the Council rediscovered, if God had not been faithful to the Jews, on what basis can Christians claim that God will be faithful to that which is revealed in Christ?

Noting the indisputable fact that "the Jews in large number" did not "accept the Gospel," and some "opposed" it

(Rom 8:28), the Council quite logically concluded with Paul that "the Jews still remain most dear to God because of their fathers, for God does not repent of the gifts he makes nor of the calls he issues" (Rom 11:28-29) (p. 28). In other words, the Covenant God made with the Jewish people is irrevocable. It has not been abrogated by the Covenant God made with Christians through Jesus Christ. In so saying, the Council contradicted the traditional claim that the Jews have been rejected by God and implicitly declared that they abide in relationship with God, independently of the Church's belief in Christ.

Noting again the historical fact that "certain authorities of the Jews and those who followed their lead, pressed for the death of Christ" (Jn 19:6), the Council repudiated the view that the Jews were collectively responsible for the death of Jesus: "What happened in his passion cannot be blamed on all Jews then living, without distinction, nor upon the Jews of today" (p. 28). Theologically, the sins of all humanity have this responsibility: "Christ in his boundless love freely underwent his passion and death because of the sins of all, so that all might attain salvation" (p. 28). Implicit in this repudiation is the rejection of the notion that Jewish suffering is God's punishment for the crime of "deicide." If Jews are not to be collectively charged with the crucifixion of Jesus, they could not have been under any divine curse and their covenantal life with God continues. *Nostra aetate* then emphasized, against the teaching of the Fathers of the Church, that "in catechetical instruction and in the preaching of God's word," the Jews "should not be presented as repudiated or cursed by God, as if such views followed from the holy scriptures" (p. 28).

To deal with the admission that Jews are saved through their own Covenant and on the Church's past efforts to convert Jews to Christianity, *Nostra aetate* introduced a future-oriented eschatology: "The Church awaits that day, known to God alone, on which all peoples will address the Lord in a single voice and 'serve Him with one accord' (Wis 3:9; cf. Is 66:23; Ps 65:4; Rom 11:11-32). In context, this is recognition that only an eschatological time will bring Jews and Christians to the common Messianic banquet. For this reason, in this pre-eschatological period, the Church no longer has any official mission for the conversion of Jews.

In view of its future-oriented eschatology, *Nostra aetate* calls for dialogue, not mission (p. 28). As Cardinal Francis Arinze, former President of the Council for Interreligious Dialogue, has repeatedly stated, "Dialogue does not aim at conversion in the sense of a change of religious allegiance, but conversion understood as self-conversion, as a greater readiness to do God's will."[3] Dialogue understood in this sense is the present Catholic goal of pursuing relations with Jews. Considering the

---

3 See, for example, his *The Church in Dialogue: Walking with Other Religions* (San Francisco: Ignatius Press, 1990), 331–32.

number of Jewish-Catholic dialogues that have taken place throughout the world over the last forty years, this call for dialogue has been very fruitful.

Nostra aetate did not deal with all the issues in the Jewish-Catholic relationship, but it was the beginning of the reversal of the Catholic attitude towards Jews and Judaism. It did not follow the typical Catholic practice of quoting and citing previous ecclesiastical and papal statements. Instead, it stepped over centuries of contemptuous teaching back to the New Testament itself.

The *Guidelines*

On 1 December 1974, roughly ten years after the Second Vatican Council, the Vatican Commission for Religious Relations with Jews issued a set of *Guidelines and Suggestions for Implementing "Nostra aetate" Article 4*. As the title implies, the document was intended to offer practical applications of *Nostra aetate*'s principles in order to promote "some concrete suggestions born of years of experience, hoping that they will help to bring into actual existence in the life of the Church the intentions expressed in the conciliar document" (p. 31). These suggestions extended the thought of *Nostra aetate* in several areas.

Whereas *Nostra aetate* speaks solely of biblical Jews, the *Guidelines* referred explicitly to the richness of post-biblical

Judaism: "The history of Judaism did not end with the destruction of Jerusalem, but rather went on to develop a tradition ... rich in religious values" (p. 35). They then called on Christians "to strive to learn by what essential traits the Jews [of today] define themselves in the light of their own religious experience" (p. 32). They noted that it is not enough for Catholics to comprehend Judaism using Christian categories. Rather, due to the validity of the Jews' own religious experiences of God, Jewish self-understanding must be the basis of Christian images of Judaism. Hence they call upon educators to explain thoroughly "those phrases and passages which Christians, if they are not well informed, might misunderstand because of prejudice" (p. 34).

Another emerging theme of the *Guidelines* concerned the Hebrew Scriptures. They pointed out that in essential ways, "the Old Testament retains its own perpetual value (cf. Second Vatican Council's Dogmatic Constitution on Divine Revelation, *Dei verbum*, Articles 14–15), since that has not been cancelled by the later interpretation of the New Testament" (p. 33). It follows from this that a Christological interpretation of the Hebrew Scriptures is not the only one. The sacred texts maintain their "perpetual value" irrespective of Christian readings.

The *Guidelines*, like *Nostra aetate*, recognize that the continuing Covenant with the Jews concerns the Church as such "since it is when 'pondering its own mystery' that it encounters the mystery of Israel" (p. 36). They recognize that Judaism is not "extrinsic" to Christianity but "intrinsic" to it.

The *Guidelines* go on to state that since Judaism and Christianity are linked at the level of their own identities, "the Old Testament and the Jewish tradition founded on it must not be set against the New Testament in such a way that the former seems to constitute a religion of justice, fear and legalism, with no appeal to the love of God and neighbor" (p. 34). This prohibition rejects what has been standard Christian practice since the patristic era. Since God is "the inspirer and author of both Testaments" (*Dei verbum*, 16), the *Guidelines* call upon all engaged in ministry to emphasize "the continuity of their faith with that of the earlier covenant" (p. 33).

With respect to the theme of promise and fulfillment, the *Guidelines* note that while the messianic promises were fulfilled in Jesus, "it is nevertheless true that we still await their perfect fulfillment in his glorious return at the end of time" (p. 33). This distinction between fulfillment and perfect fulfillment is sensitive to the Jewish claim that the Messiah has not yet come, since the Messianic Age has not yet arrived. Echoing *Nostra aetate*'s future-oriented eschatology, the nuance acknowledges that it is not enough that the Messiah has come; the Messianic Age itself must come. This sensitivity adds a note of realism, hope, and longing to the dialogue and is in keeping with the Christian faith.

The *Notes*

On 24 June 1985 the Vatican Commission for Religious Relations with the Jews issued *Notes on the Correct Way to Present the Jews and Judaism in Preaching and Catechesis in the Roman Catholic Church*.[4] The Commission saw itself as furthering the call of the *Guidelines* for precise education on Jews and Judaism, but recognized by the use of the word "Notes" that the Church was still only in the beginning steps of its new dialogue with Judaism.

While *Nostra aetate* "deplores the hatred, persecutions, and displays of antisemitism directed against the Jews at any time and from any source" (p. 28), the *Notes* recognize the urgent need for precise education on Jews and Judaism because of the continuing threat of anti-Semitism, "which is always ready to reappear under different guises" (p. 41). For this reason it observes that "the Jews and Judaism should not occupy an occasional and marginal place in catechesis: their presence there is essential and should be organically integrated" (p. 39).

Accordingly, the *Notes* proceed to discuss a number of topics. They emphasize that Christians must reclaim the full Jewishness of Jesus and not obliterate his links to the Jewish people as scholars have tried to do in the past. They point out

---

4   The page numbers refer to the text of the *Notes* as found in Fisher and Klenicki, *In Our Time*, 38–50.

that Jesus was "circumcised and presented in the Temple like any other Jew of his time (cf. Lk 2:21, 22-24)"; that he not only "extolled respect" for the law (cf. Mt 5:17-20) but also "invited obedience" to it (cf. Mt 8:4); that the rhythm of his life was marked by the observance of Jewish feasts, even from infancy (cf. Lk 2:41-50; Jn 2:13; 7:10, etc.); and that he taught in synagogues, "as did the disciples even after the Resurrection (cf. e.g., Acts 2:46; 3:1; 21:26, etc.)" (p. 44).

The *Notes* were the first Vatican document to explore the relationship between Jesus and the Pharisees (pp. 45–46). They make clear that Jesus did not condemn all Pharisees as hypocrites, that his relations with them "were not always polemical," that it was the Pharisees who warned Jesus of the risks he was running (Lk 13:31), that Jesus praised some of them (Mk 12:34) and even ate with them (Lk 7:36, 14:1), and that it is "noteworthy that the Pharisees are not mentioned in the accounts of the passion." They stress that Jesus shared "some pharisaic doctrines: the resurrection of the body, forms of piety like almsgiving, prayer, fasting (cf. Mt 6:1-18), and the practice of addressing God as Father." In sum, the *Notes* make clear that a "negative picture of the Pharisees is likely to be inaccurate and unjust" (p. 45). This point is important for dialogue, since negative traits ascribed to the Pharisees are likely to be imputed to the Jews as a whole.

When the *Notes* discuss anti-Judaism in the Gospels, they recognize that the New Testament references that are "hostile or less than favorable to the Jews" do not reflect the teaching of Jesus but "the conflicts between the nascent Church and the Jewish community ... long after the time of Jesus" (p. 46). They specify that in the Gospel of John, the formula "the Jews" varies with the context, referring sometimes to the "leaders of the Jews," at other times to "adversaries of Jesus," and at no time "arraigns the Jewish people as such" (pp. 46, 34).

The *Notes* even acknowledge that "the Liturgy of the Word in its own structure originates in Judaism. The Prayer of the Hours and other liturgical texts and formularies have their parallels in Judaism as do the very formulas of our most venerable prayers, among them the Our Father" (p. 48).

The *Notes* go on to discuss the relationship between the Hebrew Scriptures and the New Testament in the context of biblical typology, marking the first treatment of this issue in ecclesiastical documents concerning Jews and Judaism. The discussion begins with an acknowledgment that traditionally, biblical typology was understood as "reading the Old Testament as a preparation and ... foreshadowing of the New Testament, in which Christ ... is the key and point of reference to the [Hebrew] Scriptures" (p. 42). The apparent difficulty with this hermeneutic is the danger that a purely Christological reading of the Bible tends to deny the validity of any other approach. The *Notes* therefore emphasize that this typological reading "should not lead [Christians] to forget that the Hebrew Scriptures retain its own value as Revelation"

(p. 43) and that Christians can benefit from the traditions of Jewish reading (p. 43).

The *Notes* proceed to frame the question of typology with reference to the Church and Judaism as they both await their definitive perfecting and final consummation in the End Time (p. 42). This procedure allows for an alternative model for relating the Hebrew Scriptures and the New Testament. It does so by utilizing the movement towards a future-oriented eschatology present in *Nostra aetate* and is in keeping with the theme of promise and fulfillment found in the *Guidelines*. It asserts that typology

> signifies reaching towards the accomplishment of the divine plan, when "God will be all in all." (1 Cor 15:28). This holds true for the Church which, realized already in Christ, still awaits its definitive perfecting as the Body of Christ. The fact that the Body of Christ is still tending towards its full stature (cf. Eph 4:12-19) takes nothing from the value of being a Christian. So also the calling of the patriarchs and the Exodus from Egypt do not lose their importance and value in God's design from being at the same time intermediate stages (cf., e.g. *Nostra aetate*, 4). (p. 43)

By referring to the unrealized aspects of salvation and to the future eschaton, the *Notes* thus propose a typological approach that conceives of the Hebrew Scriptures, the Christ event, and the life of the Church as all adumbrations of the great eschatological future, when the fulfillment of God's design will find its final consummation. This procedure significantly relativized the typology's power to one hermeneutical approach. The *Notes* maintain that neither the Church nor the Jewish people exist for themselves but are all called to live out God's ultimate purpose.

Such a future eschatological perspective enabled the *Notes* to say that Catholics and Jews share a mission to prepare the world for the Messiah:

> In underlying the eschatological dimension of Christianity, we shall reach a greater awareness that the people of God of the Old and New Testaments are tending towards a like end in the future: the coming or return of the Messiah – even if they start from two different points of view. It is more clearly understood that the person of the Messiah is not only a point of division for the people of God but also a point of convergence. (p. 43)

The *Notes* call on both Jews and Christians to bear joint witness to "our common hope in Him who is the master of history. We must accept our responsibility to prepare the world for the coming of the Messiah by working together for social justice.... To this we are driven ... by a common hope for the kingdom of God" (p. 44).

Here we have additional evidence from a Roman Catholic document that the recognition of the "not yet" or unfinished dimension of Christian expectations accompanies the affirmation of the continuing Covenant between God and the people of Israel. This recognition enables one to stress the joint witness of Jews and Christians to the world; to acknowledge an authentic and ongoing Jewish mission to the world that is not a preparation for Christ; and to defer the thorny issue of Jewish recognition of the divine sonship of Jesus out of the present temporal frame and into the eschatological future.

For the first time in a Vatican document, the *Notes* raised the issues of the land and the Holocaust, although in a preliminary way. Recalling the admission of the *Guidelines* that the "history of Israel did not end in 70 A.D.," it observes that this history continued "especially in a Diaspora which allowed Israel to carry to the whole world a witness – often heroic – of its fidelity to the one God and to 'exalt Him in the presence of the living' (Tb 13:4), while preserving the memory of the land of their forefathers at the heart of their hope" (pp. 48–49).

The *Notes* invite Christians "to understand this religious attachment [to the land] which finds its root in the Biblical tradition." They add that "The permanence of Israel is a historic fact ... to be interpreted within God's design." It exhorted Christians "to rid themselves of the traditional idea of the [wandering Jew], of a people *punished,* preserved as a *living argument* for Christian apologetic." They reiterated that the Jews remain "a chosen people, 'the pure olive tree on which were grafted the branches of the wild olive which are the Gentiles'" (p. 49). The affirmation of the *Guidelines* (p. 32) that Christians are to recognize Jewish self-understanding of their own religious experience includes the Jewish attachment to the land. In this connection, the establishment of formal diplomatic relations between the Holy See and the State of Israel in 1993 is noteworthy.

The *Notes* encourage catechesis on the Holocaust when they say, "Catechesis should help in understanding the meaning for the Jews of the Shoah during the years 1939–1945, and its consequences" (p. 49). Perhaps because the issue of the Holocaust was raised only in a preliminary way, the Vatican issued a document on the Holocaust in 1998. This document, *We Remember: A Reflection on the Shoah*,[5] made a distinction between anti-Judaism, based on Christian theories of triumphalism, and modern anti-Semitism, based on a pseudo-scientific racialism set in Nazi ideology. It then acknowledged that while Christian anti-Judaism differed profoundly from racial anti-Semitism, Christian anti-Judaism did pave the way for the successful spread of anti-Semitism through Christian teaching that had for centuries pinpointed the Jews as an alien other in Christian society (pp. 62, 66). Put another way, the document acknowledged that Christian

---

5 The page numbers refer to the text of *We Remember: A Reflection on the Shoah* as found in *Catholic Jewish Relations: Documents from the Holy See* (London: Catholic Truth Society, 1999).

anti-Judaism did contribute to the persecution of the Jews during the Holocaust, but claimed that it was not a sufficient cause. Without it, the Holocaust would probably never have happened. But other causes – sociological, economic, historical, and ideological – must also be considered if we are to have a sufficient explanation for what happened.

It is dialogical to note here what *Dabru Emet*,[6] a Jewish statement on Christians and Christianity published in September 2000, had to say concerning Christian involvement in the Holocaust. *Dabru Emet* stated explicitly that "Nazism is not a Christian phenomenon. Without the long history of Christian anti-Judaism and Christian violence against Jews, Nazi ideology could not have taken hold nor could it have been carried out, but Nazism itself was not an inevitable outcome of Christianity." This Jewish statement resonates with the Vatican statement.

Dominus Iesus

The declaration *Dominus Iesus*,[7] published on 6 August 2000 by the Congregation for the Doctrine of the Faith, sparked some misunderstandings of the Jewish-Catholic

---

6 For the text of *Dabru Emet*, see Tikva Frymer-Kensky et al., eds., *Christianity in Jewish Terms* (Boulder, CO: Westview Press, 2000), xvii-xx.

7 The page numbers refer to the text of *Dominus Iesus* as found in Stephen J. Pope and Charles Heflung, eds., *Sic et Non: Encountering Dominus Iesus* (Maryknoll, NY: Orbis Books, 2002), 3–23.

relationship. This document deals with interreligious dialogue between Christianity and the "non-Christian" religions and argues against some Christian theologians who advocate a pluralistic vision of religion (pp. 5–6). Some scholars seem to have assumed that Judaism, being clearly "non-Christian," was seen by the Congregation as simply one among many "non-Christian religions," which *Dominus Iesus* deems to be "gravely deficient" (p. 21). The presumption led them to view the document as a backward step in a concerted effort to overturn the Catholic-Jewish relationship of the recent decades.

A closer look at *Dominus Iesus* shows that the document's argument against a pluralistic vision of religion is based on the distinction between "faith," as a response to divine revelation as we have it in the sacred scriptures, and "belief," as the human search for God and human religious wisdom, which it discerns in non-Christian religions (pp. 7–8). Now the key question on which everything depends with regard to Judaism is where the authors of *Dominus Iesus* put Judaism. Is it belief? In this case it would be "gravely deficient." Or is it in its own right a "faith," a response to divine revelation? Judaism is clearly a non-Christian religion, and it is true that *Dominus Iesus* does not comment on Judaism one way or another. On the surface, it is a reasonable assumption that Judaism falls in the category of world religions. But in Catholic thinking, such a conclusion is wrong. As we have seen in our review of *Nostra aetate*, the *Guidelines*, and the *Notes*, Judaism, unlike other non-Christian religions, is a response to divine revelation as given in the Old Testament. Indeed, *Dominus Iesus* specifically acknowledges that the Hebrew Scriptures are a divine revelation, in contrast to the sacred books of other religions, which it regards as mere human wisdom. It does so by stating that "The Church reserves the designation of inspired texts to the canonical books of the Old and New Testament, since they are inspired by the Holy Spirit" (pp. 8–9). "The misunderstanding [that Judaism is just another world religion] can be avoided if the declaration is read and interpreted – as any magisterial document should be – in the larger context of all official documents and declarations, which are by no means cancelled, revoked or nullified by this document."[8] Read in this wider context, Judaism remains unique among the world's religions, because, as *Nostra aetate* states, "it is the root of that good olive tree unto which have been grafted the wild olive branches of the Gentiles" (Rom 11:17-24) (p. 27).

Pope Benedict XVI, while still Prefect of the Congregation for the Doctrine of the Faith, clarified this issue in his article "The Heritage of Abraham," published in *L'Osservatore Romano* on 29 December 2000. He wrote: "It is evident that the dialogue for us Christians with the Jews stands on a different level with regard to the dialogue with other religions. The

---

8   Walter Kasper, "The Good Olive Tree," *America* Vol. 185, No. 7 (17 September 2001): 2.

faith witnessed in the Bible of the Jews, the Old Testament of Christians, is for us not a different religion but the foundation of our own faith."[9]

Dominus Iesus also raised Jewish suspicion when it spoke of evangelization and mission (p. 4) with respect to the world's religions. The misunderstanding arose since many scholars were unaware that these are technical terms. Evangelization in an official Church document "implies presence and witness, dialogue and social work."[10] And dialogue, as we recall, is not for the sake of converting non-believers to the Catholic faith, but for converting all partners in dialogue to a deeper relationship with God.

On the other hand, "the term mission, in its proper sense, refers to conversion from false gods and idols to the true and one God ... thus mission, in this strict sense, cannot be used with regard to Jews, who believe in the true and one God."[11] This explains why, since *Nostra aetate*, there does not exist any missionary organization for Jews. There is dialogue, not mission.

This interpretation of *Dominus Iesus* is based on that of Cardinal Walter Kasper, the current President of the Pontifical Commission for Religious Relations with the Jews. The

---

9 Joseph Ratzinger, "New Vision of the Relationship Between the Church and the Jews," *Origins* Vol. 30, No. 35 (15 February 2001): 566.

10 Kasper, "The Good Olive Tree," 4.

11 Ibid.

declaration, while not on the order of the Congregation for the Doctrine of the Faith which it interprets, is nonetheless not simply another opinion. It was issued on a formal occasion when the Cardinal was speaking for the Catholic Church to the Jewish people. It was published in the Catholic journal *America* (17 September 2001)[12] and has been twice repeated by His Eminence on occasions when he was representing the view of the Holy See to the Jewish Community, in Jerusalem and in Montevideo. So it represents the definitive statement by the Holy See of the meaning of *Dominus Iesus* for Catholic-Jewish relations.

Unsettled Questions

Having reaffirmed that the Church teaches that the Jews are saved through their own Covenant, Cardinal Kasper, in an address on the relationship of the Old and New Covenant, given in December [2004] at the Centre for the Study of Jewish-Christian Relations at Cambridge in the United Kingdom, admitted that this acknowledgment leaves the Church with unsettled questions. He asked: "How can the thesis of the continuing Covenant with the Jews be reconciled with the claim of the uniqueness and universality of salvation through Christ? ... Can or should we replace the substitution

---

12 See note 8 above.

theory with a dualism in the sense of a coexistence of the old and new Covenant, or even a pluralism in the sense of a number of covenants?"[13] This last question is a provocative invitation to explore the implications of the Church's recognition of the Jewish Covenant for the Muslim-Christian dialogue, since Islam is a monotheistic religion not unrelated to the Judeo-Christian tradition.

Vatican II did say that God's plan of salvation "... includes the Muslims, who, professing to hold the faith of Abraham, along with us, adore the one and merciful God" (Dogmatic Constitution on the Church, *Lumen gentium*, 16; also *Nostra aetate*, 3). Pope John Paul II expanded on this point in his discourse to the Catholic community in Ankara (3 December 1979) when he said, "They have, like you, the faith of Abraham in the one, almighty, and merciful God."[14] In his message to the President of Pakistan (23 February 1981) he referred to the faith of Abraham as that to which "Christians, Muslims and Jews eagerly link their own."[15] In Lisbon (14 May 1982),

---

13 Cardinal Walter Kasper, "The Relationship of the Old and New Covenant as One of the Central Issues in the Jewish-Christian Dialogue," Centre for the Study of Jewish Christian Relations, Cambridge, UK, December 2004. Available online at http://www.cjcr.cam.ac.uk/centre/covenant/pres-index.html. (Accessed October 2, 2006)

14 John Paul II, "Moslems and Christians: The Pope in Ankara," *Origins* Vol. 9, No. 26 (13 December 1979): 419.

15 John Paul II, "Islam and Christianity," *Origins* Vol. 10, No. 37 (26 February 1981): 592.

he said: "And Abraham, our common forefather, teaches all – Christians, Jews, and Muslims – to follow the path of mercy and love."[16] And in his address to Muslims at Casablanca (19 August 1985) he said: "Your God and ours is the same, and we are brothers and sisters in the faith of Abraham."[17]

It can be argued that the Pope's acknowledgment that Judaism, Christianity, and Islam are three parallel expressions of the faith of Abraham is an implicit admission that Muslims, like Jews, are saved in their own way as heirs of the faith of Abraham. For just as the Mosaic Covenant is still in force for the Jews, so also the faith of Abraham retains its validity. This admission is in keeping with the teaching of *Nostra aetate* 4, on the role of the patriarchs in salvation and with the teaching of Paul that "the gifts and calling of God are irrevocable" (Rom 11:29).

Furthermore, with the acceptance of Abraham as our common forefather, Abraham does not replace Jesus, since only faith in the risen Lord makes Christians children of Abraham. As Paul says, "If you belong to Christ, then you

---

16   John Paul II, cited by Thomas Michel, "Islamo-Christian Dialogue: Reflections on the Recent Teachings of the Church," *Bulletin* (Secretariatus pro non-Christianis) 20/2 (1985): 184. On a Christian theology of Islam, see Ovey N. Mohammed, *Muslim-Christians, Past, Present, Future* (Maryknoll, NY: Orbis Books, 1999), 59–61.

17   Jan van Lin, "Mission and Dialogue: God and Jesus Christ," in *Muslims and Christians in Europe: Breaking New Ground: Essays in Honor of Jan Slomp*, eds. Gé Speelman, Jan van Lin, and Dick Mulder (Kampden: Uitgeverij Kok, 1993), 153, 167.

are Abraham's offspring, heirs to the promise" (Gal 3:29). Neither does Abraham replace the Quran, for the Quran is necessary to make the religion of Abraham concrete for the Muslim community. Members of each community are children of Abraham according to their own self-understanding. And on a more sober note, being children of Abraham does not exempt Christians, Muslims, and Jews from disputes, conflicts, and misunderstandings. These things do occur among brothers and sisters in a normal family.

Conclusion

However the Church eventually settles the unsettled questions of the Jewish-Catholic relationship, the way forward will surely be marked by numerous obstacles, detours, and setbacks. But in the opening decade of the twenty-first century, we can see more clearly that we are sojourners together on the way to the future. The way in which we choose to travel that road will have profound consequences both for communities and for dialogue with the world religions. Fortunately, as we celebrate the fortieth anniversary of *Nostra aetate*, there are already positive and encouraging signs of progress. Patterns of encounter that once alienated are being replaced by patterns that seek to take into account the mistakes of the past, the needs of the present, and the promises envisioned by the future.

3

NOSTRA AETATE AND DABRU EMET

David Novak
J. Richard and Dorothy Shiff Professor of Jewish Studies
Department and Centre for the Study of Religion
University of Toronto

In this volume we are commemorating the most remarkable document to have emerged from the Second Vatican Council, the "Declaration on the Church's Relation to Non-Christian Religions" (*Nostra aetate*). And, of course, the most remarkable part of this most remarkable document is the part that deals with the relationship of the Catholic Church and the Jewish people, and the Catholic Church and Judaism.

In *Nostra aetate*, the Catholic Church affirmed two main points about the Jewish people and the Judaism that give the Jewish people its unique and indelible identity in the world.

The first point is that the Catholic Church and Christianity in general enjoy a relationship with Judaism and the Jewish people that is unlike its relationship with any other people or religion in the world. That is because it is no accident that Jesus, who for all Christians is the Christ or Messiah and the second person of the Trinity or the Triune God, was born a Jew, lived his entire life as a faithful Jew among Jews, and died as a faithful Jew. Moreover, since all Christians, and certainly all Catholics, have always affirmed that Jesus was resurrected from the dead on Easter, it cannot be denied by those who affirm this dogma that the body of Jesus so resurrected is a Jewish body. That is, it is a body born of a Jewish mother and is a circumcised body forever bearing in its flesh God's Covenant with Abraham and all his descendants, both those born into the Covenant or those reborn into the Covenant via conversion to Judaism. As such, when Catholics take communion during the celebration of the Mass, are they not by virtue of their own theology merging their own bodies with the Jewish body of Jesus?

By emphasizing the true origins of Christianity, both spiritual and physical, *Nostra aetate* held that the Church as a people must look to her living roots to know from where it has come and to where it is yet to go in its journey in and through this world. And, along these lines, the words of the person who might be considered the first Christian theologian, Paul of Tarsus, are worth quoting. Paul's struggle with the roots of what came to be known as Christianity is still the struggle of every serious Christian thinker who has come after him.

> If the dough offered as first fruits is holy, so is the whole lump; and if the root is holy, so are the branches. But if some of the branches were broken off, and you, a wild olive shoot, were grafted in their place to share the richness of the olive tree, do not boast over the branches. If you do boast, remember it is not you that support the root, but the root that supports you. (Rom 11:16-18, Revised Standard Version)

And, in case the point of this elaborate metaphor has been lost on his Gentile readers, Paul makes it more explicit: "But as regards election they are beloved for the sake of their forefathers. For the gifts and the call of God are irrevocable" (Rom 11:28-29).

Like any healthy branch, Christianity requires the tree onto which it has been grafted to be healthy and robust. But whenever the branch attempts to replace its tree, it thereby loses its life-giving roots. Thus Paul clearly taught, and *Nostra aetate* even more clearly reiterated, that Christianity – the Church – is rooted in God's everlasting Covenant with Abraham and his descendants. When the Church forgets this, as it has often done throughout its history, Christianity becomes rootless and without origin. So, in fact, even otherwise anti-Jewish Christian thinkers have had to acknowledge the necessity for the continuing existence of the Jewish people in order for Christianity to be able to point to its ever-present origin in the world, which makes it able to resist the charge that it has in fact invented its own origins in a by-now irretrievable, mythological past. Thus, by emphasizing its Jewish origins in *Nostra aetate*, the teaching authority (*magisterium*) of the Catholic Church reiterates traditional Christian teaching, but with a more positive force than it had for a long time, perhaps with a force that it has never had before. In the past, the need for Christianity to affirm its Jewish origins (and for these origins not to be overcome and designated passé) was often fulfilled out of a sense of necessity, but in *Nostra aetate* it seems that this Christian affirmation and reaffirmation of Jewish origin is now done as something desirable, something valuable for its own sake.

The second point that *Nostra aetate* makes is that God's Covenant with the Jewish people, like the existence of the Jewish people themselves, is everlasting. On this point, the Catholic Church was deciding in favour of one side in the centuries-old debate within Christianity over *supersessionism*. There have always been Christian theologians who have taught that because the Jewish people have rejected the messianic claims of Jesus and because their rejection is based on Judaism, God has replaced the Jewish people with the Church as Israel, the true people of the Covenant, and God has replaced Judaism with Christianity as the one and only true faith. In this view, Judaism, as the way Jews live according to God's Covenant now, is illegitimate in the eyes of God: Judaism no longer has any theological validity. Indeed, in this view, Jews are practising a false religion. Obviously, there can be no real dialogue with Christians who hold this view of Judaism and the Jewish people.

The practical corollary of this supersessionism has most often been the Christian attempt to proselytize Jews, that is, to try to convince Jews that their only fulfillment or salvation lies in becoming Christians. For the proselytizers, Jews who remain within Judaism are doomed to being totally rejected by God. Indeed, overt proselytizing usually requires that one tries to convince the object of such efforts how bad, how hopeless or baseless, is their present situation. In the case of Jews, they must realize therefore the only remedy for their existential plight is to accept what the Christian missionary is offering as replacement for their discredited Judaism. Of course, that has also characterized Christian proselytizing of pagans. Nevertheless, Christian supersessionists have tried to make Jews feel that their situation is especially bad since, unlike most pagans who might never have had any contact with Jesus, Jews should repent – literally, "return from" – their rejection of Jesus.

In line with this kind of Christian supersessionism, there has been the charge of deicide. The most extreme kinds of Christian supersessionism have taught that instead of accepting Jesus as their messiah (and more), the Jews killed him. The political corollary of this theological anti-Judaism has often been specifically Christian anti-Semitism. In its milder forms, Christian anti-Semitism has advocated civil discrimination against those Jews who have refused to convert to Christianity. In its more extreme forms, Christian anti-Semitism has advocated such things as banishment of unconverted Jews (for example, the expulsion of the Jews from Spain in 1492 under the reign of Ferdinand and Isabella). In its most extreme form, as practised especially during the First Crusade, Jews have been given the gruesome choice of conversion to Christianity or death.

To be sure, supersessionism need not lead to charges of deicide or the advocacy of overt oppression and violence against Jews. Nevertheless, when these corollaries are drawn, supersessionists have little or no argument against them, even when it has been obvious that Christian theology was being cynically used by those whose political agendas were anything but theological in essence. The most that supersessionists of this kind (that is, those who are liberals politically) could argue for is that the civil rights of any human being ought not be violated, and that includes Jews, and that the state not impose a religion – even Christianity – on anyone, especially not on any of its own citizens. I might add, however, that even this kind of Christian supersessionist can come up with some good theological arguments against Nazi-type racist anti-Semitism that offers the Jews no hope in the face of Nazi-type racists intent on killing them, irrespective of whether they remain Jews, convert to Christianity, or renounce any and all religion.

Nostra aetate has pulled the rug out from under even the milder kind of supersessionism by rejecting the charge of deicide against the Jews. I might add that although my childhood experiences with Christians in the 1940s and 1950s were quite good, for the most part, I remember all too well at least two occasions when I was called a "Christ-killer" – and this while I was on the run from the fists of those who were shouting it at me. I dare say, though, that since *Nostra aetate* has filtered down to the mass of ordinary Catholics, there are hardly any Jewish children today who would be called "Christ-killer" by any churchgoing Catholic.

Needless to say, contemporary Jews have very realistic concerns over anti-Semitism. For that reason alone, perceptive Jews should take notice when any group of Christians seems to be moving away from supersessionism. Furthermore, one can see the Vatican's diplomatic recognition of the State of Israel, during the pontificate of the late (revered and beloved) Pope John Paul II, as being an unanticipated result of the rejection of supersessionism by the Catholic Church. Just as the Church now recognizes the right of Jews to remain within Judaism, so does the Church now recognize the right of the Jewish people to have a sovereign Jewish state in the land of Israel.

From my own study of Christian theology over the years, there is only one kind of supersessionism (if that is even the right word for it) Christian theology cannot deny without giving up Christian truth claims. That is, Christians cannot help but regard Christianity to have a better grasp of the ultimate truth of God's Covenant with Israel than does Judaism. However, Jews can hardly be offended by this kind of supersessionism, since we claim that Judaism has a better grasp of that same truth than does Christianity. Here the difference is between *good and better* rather than between *good and bad*, let alone than between *true and false*. In fact, Jews can object to this kind of supersessionism only when Christians use it in overtly proselytizing Jews. However, one of the most significant practical effects of *Nostra aetate* has been that the Catholic Church no longer directly targets Jews for proselytization. Of course, the Catholic Church will accept converts from wherever, including those coming from the Jewish people. But, then again, we Jews also accept converts from wherever, including those who come from the Church. And, just as Catholics need not denigrate the religious background of those who desire to become Christian, so Jews need not denigrate the religious background of anyone who desires to convert to Judaism and become a member of the Jewish people.

Like any such significant historical document, *Nostra aetate* has a past, a present, and, it is hoped, a future. It is important that we look into the past, present, and future of *Nostra aetate*. But first I would like to recount some of my own involvement in its past and present.

Nostra aetate was issued by the Catholic Church as one of the official documents of Vatican Council II in 1965. But, actually, the Jewish involvement in the creation of this document formally began in 1962, when an invitation was addressed to my late revered and beloved teacher, Professor Abraham Joshua Heschel, to come to the Vatican to meet with Augustin Cardinal Bea, who was in charge of the Vatican congregation dealing with other religions. I was a student of Professor Heschel at that time and part of a special program with three other students at the Jewish Theological Seminary of America in New York City. Professor Heschel realized the tremendous importance of this invitation to visit Cardinal Bea and actively consult with him because the idea for Vatican Council II had already been promoted by the late revered and beloved Pope John XXIII. Professor Heschel, being not only a great theologian but also an astute student of Jewish history, appreciated the momentous significance of a document that was likely to express the Church's changed view of the Jewish people and Judaism. So he accepted this invitation quite willingly but with a good deal of trepidation. He discussed his hopes and concerns with those of us who were then his closest students.

When word emerged of Professor Heschel's visit with Cardinal Bea, there surfaced in the Jewish community a number of criticisms and even protests that this leading Jewish theologian was actually entering into such publicized discussions with high church officials. A number of reservations and censures were made for a variety of reasons. One such reason was that this seemed to be a revival of the medieval disputations, when Jews were basically summoned by Christian monarchs to debate with Christian clergy about the respective merits and demerits of Judaism vis-à-vis Christianity. Inevitably, Jews emerged from these disputations as the losers, even if intellectually they may have won the arguments, simply because of their impoverished political situation in comparison with the Church. That was the first such critique of Professor Heschel's entrance into these discussions.

The second critique was based upon the fear of proselytization. This is a very real fear; Christians have very intensely attempted to proselytize Jews for much of our common 2,000-year history. The concern was that this was one more effort to proselytize Jews, even if it was being done more subtly than it had been done in the past.

The third critique was that Jews ought not to enter into interreligious discussions with any other religion. In other words, if Christians were planning on changing their doctrines, that was their business. But why should Jews become involved in what was essentially an internal Christian debate? In fact, it was even argued that if Jews were perceived of as getting certain favours, considerations, and alterations in negative attitudes from the Church, would not the Church somehow require that Jews change their own theology as well in return for such favours, considerations, and alterations in Jewish negative attitudes towards Christians and Christianity? Professor Heschel was aware of all of these criticisms and knew some of the prominent Jewish scholars who made them; he was even personally hurt by them. Nevertheless, he proceeded and engaged in an extraordinary series of conversations with Cardinal Bea and the late Pope Paul VI. Interestingly enough, the first meeting between Professor Heschel and Cardinal Bea (conducted in German, I might add, which was Cardinal Bea's native tongue and Professor Heschel's adopted tongue, having come to Germany from Poland in the late 1920s to pursue a doctorate at the University of Berlin) was over the Jewish and Christian interpretations of the Song of Songs. The Song of Songs is ostensibly a series of erotic love lyrics. The rationale for including these erotic love lyrics in the biblical canon is that they are taken to be allegories of God's love of Israel in Jewish scriptural exegesis and Christ's love for the Church in Christian scriptural exegesis. This is significant because almost all the major contacts between Jewish and Christian thinkers before this great encounter were conducted on the basis of diplomatic and political concerns. Professor Heschel realized wisely that, as he famously put it, "interfaith dialogue begins with faith," with authentic faith on the side of each of the parties entering the dialogue.

Nostra aetate was issued in 1965, and one can see how tremendously it influenced Catholic attitudes towards the Jewish people and towards Judaism in a number of ways. I was especially happy to note this in 1985, when the twentieth anniversary of *Nostra aetate* was celebrated in Rome during a conference at the Angelicum (the Dominican university where Pope John Paul II studied for his doctorate), where I had the great honour to be the main Jewish speaker. In my talk, I noted that it was clear that although there were no doubt still a number of Christian anti-Semites in the world, Christians, and especially Catholics, were no longer receiving any warrant for their anti-Semitism from the teaching of the Church. The second point was that even though the Catholic Church accepts converts and even engages in proselytization, since the release of *Nostra aetate* specific missions for targeting Jews for conversion are no longer being supported by the Catholic Church. The Church, like the Jewish people, accepts converts from anywhere, but it no longer targets Jews for purposes of conversion. Finally, the third point, which was not known in 1965, was the Vatican's diplomatic recognition of the State of Israel. I remember the audience that twelve of us had with Pope John Paul II in November 1986. Nathan Perlmutter, then head of the Anti-Defamation League of B'nai Brith, made a formal presentation to the Pope requesting that at long last the Vatican recognize the State of Israel. At the time, the Pope quite diplomatically smiled and said nothing in return. Nevertheless, something was clearly in the works. Those of us present sensed that the Pope already knew what Nathan Perlmutter was going to say and Nathan Perlmutter already knew that the Pope could not yet say anything in public. I think we can also attribute at least some of the impetus for this process on the part of the Vatican to *Nostra aetate*.

In terms of *Nostra aetate* in the present day, it has very much stimulated a desire among Jews, in our own way, to present a Jewish view of Christians and Christianity, just as *Nostra aetate* presented a Christian, specifically Catholic, view of Jews and Judaism. In fact, this is something that the Christian theologians, with whom some of us had been engaged in long and fruitful dialogue, have requested from us, and a number of us have considered this to be a legitimate request. In 1997, four Jewish theologians – Peter Ochs of the University of Virginia, Michael Signer of University of Notre Dame, Professor Tikva Frymer-Kensky of the University of Chicago, and me – came together to produce such a document. It was a kind of Jewish *Nostra aetate*, which we finally titled *Dabru Emet*, taken from a biblical phrase from the book of Zechariah (8:16) meaning "to speak the truth."

Two of the main points of our document, which was issued in September 2000 in a full-page advertisement in the *New*

York Times, were that Christians are not idolaters, even though this is a very much debated point in Jewish theology, just as supersessionism is a very much debated point in Christian theology. There are basically two strands of thinking on that question in the Jewish tradition; we opted for the strand that teaches that Jews and Christians worship the same God but in very different ways. The second major point of *Dabru Emet* was our recognition that Christians and Jews share the same book, which is the Hebrew Bible or the Old Testament, and indeed we base all of our respective authoritative claims on that book.

The first point about Jews and Christians worshipping the same God bothered several more traditional Jewish thinkers, who emphasized the strand of Jewish theology that seems to hold that Christians in fact worship another god. Our answer to them has been that we emphasize the strand of Jewish theology that definitely holds that Christians are genuine monotheists, regardless of how much we Jews might think that their form of monotheistic worship is inappropriate for Jews; being for us "strange worship" (*avodah zarah*). Indeed, their worship cannot be our worship; yet it is not the worship of a "strange god" (*el zar*).

The second point on the authority of Scripture, or the Hebrew Bible, for both Judaism and Christianity bothered several more liberal Jewish thinkers, because of what they perceived to be its "authoritarian" overtones. (I can well imagine more liberal Christian thinkers being similarly bothered by *Dabru Emet*.) Our response to them was that – whether for Jews or for Christians – the Bible is not *Scripture* unless it has authority. By "authority" I mean that which can be the basis of non-negotiable commandments. And, as "religious authority," the Bible is the basis from which Jews and Christians discern what God's will is for them. This religious authority in both Judaism and Christianity makes theological and moral claims on Jews and on Christians. (There are deeper differences between Jews and Christians over the theological claims derived from Scripture than differences over the moral claims derived from Scripture.) Thus no theological claim or moral claim has any real authority unless it is based on Scripture or, minimally, it does not contradict Scripture. That is as true of the claims made in the New Testament as it is true of the claims made in the Talmud. Furthermore, "authoritarianism" should not be confused with authentic authority.

Whereas authoritarianism is politically unnecessary and morally and theologically odious, authentic authority is both necessary and desirable on political, moral, and theological grounds. In fact, authoritarianism is a cynical parody of authentic authority. Authentic authority in Judaism and in Christianity is based on Scripture and is expressed through rational persuasion of the members of the religious community who are being authoritatively claimed. Conversely, inauthentic authority or authoritarianism is not based on

Scripture and is not expressed through rational persuasion of the members of the religious community upon whom it is being imposed. Authoritarianism appears when leaders of religious communities impose their authority on others by virtue of who they are rather than what they are saying. The claims made by authoritarians are made on the basis of their political power rather than on the basis of their persuasive reasoning. That is why, moreover, we, the authors of and signatories to *Dabru Emet*, did not claim any personal authority for ourselves or for our public statement. We attempted only to persuade those willing to listen to our arguments. We have even invited our critics to argue against us (something, at least so far, we have not yet heard) rather than simply dismissing or ridiculing us.

Our reiteration of scriptural authority and philosophically astute theological reasoning attempts to avoid the extremes of antinomianism or religious anarchism of those to the left of us and the authoritarianism of those to the right of us. And, along these lines, I might add my own appreciation of the encyclicals of the late Pope John Paul II. Although the Pope could have simply spoken in the name of his own papal authority (*ex cathedra* or "from the throne" of Peter), he always went to extraordinary lengths to invoke Scripture and engage in careful reasoning when making his authoritative points to the members of the Church. In fact, reading these encyclicals often reminded me of some of the great rabbinic responses (*teshuvot*) that treat similar questions of faith and morals with similar learning and intelligence.

These two propositions, concerning monotheism and religious authority, caused some degree of controversy in the Jewish community. The Jewish reaction to our statement was one of mild criticism, mild acceptance. A large segment of the official Jewish community basically ignored our statement – apparently, improved relations between Jews and Christians is not high on their political agenda. Nonetheless, our statement has been translated into at least eight languages, and I am proud to say that one of those languages is Hebrew. *Dabru Emet* was very well received several years ago at a conference held in Jerusalem that was specifically designed for Israeli Jews.

There is an obligation for those of us who wrote *Dabru Emet*, and the almost 200 Jewish scholars and leaders who signed on to the statement, to make sure that the fact of *Dabru Emet* and its important content be made known to a much wider number of Jews than those at present. This is the "present" of *Nostra aetate*, *Dabru Emet* being to a certain extent a response to it.

As for the future of *Nostra aetate/Dabru Emet*, there are a number of questions waiting on the horizon. I personally think that the most important task for Jewish thinkers and scholars and Catholic thinkers and scholars is to work out what I might call our common moral agenda. This common moral agenda, rooted in the Hebrew Bible, affirms that every human being is created in the image of God, what Jews call the *tselem elohim* and Christians call *imago dei*. This theological truth, which we both uphold out of the same source, is the basis for the dignity of the human person, something that Pope John Paul II so forcefully emphasized throughout his life: the dignity of the human person, the dignity of human society, the dignity of the human family and all that that entails. There is much work to be done in that area. In my own case, I have tried to work in that sphere, especially in the pro-life movement, which advocates that all human life from conception to natural human death be protected and not destroyed in any way for any reason. These are the questions that have arisen out of the past of *Nostra aetate*. They continue to press into the future. The future of *Nostra aetate* and *Dabru Emet* insists that each of us persist in the work of our own respective faith communities. I think the future holds a number of tremendous challenges, but with God's help, it also holds tremendous opportunities for both of us, in our own respective ways and together, to bear faithful witness to the Lord God of Israel, even as each of our communities believes itself to be God's elect, His chosen people.

4

ISSUES FOR FUTURE CATHOLIC-JEWISH RELATIONS

Edward Idris Cardinal Cassidy
President Emeritus of the Pontifical Council
for Promoting Christian Unity
and the Vatican's Commission for Religious Relations
with the Jews

Introduction

Forty years have passed since the Second Vatican Council presented the document *Nostra aetate* to the Catholic Church and the world. One section of that document, Article 4, dealt specifically with Catholic-Jewish relations and has resulted in a radical change in their regard. Other essays in this volume describe the past and present situation in these relations; in this essay, I wish to look to the future.

When presenting my book on rediscovering Vatican II – *Ecumenism and Interreligious Dialogue*[1] – Cardinal Walter Kasper, President of the Vatican's Commission for Religious Relations with the Jews (CRRJ), acknowledged with joy the progress made over the past forty years but remarked that we are still "at the beginning of the beginning."

A reading of the story of Catholic-Jewish relations over the past forty years presents us with a useful background for our reflections on the future. In the first period of official contacts between the Vatican Commission and the Jewish community, represented mainly through the International Jewish Committee for Interreligious Consultations (IJCIC), most attention had to be given to clearing the decks. Prejudices had to be removed, misunderstandings cleared up, unfortunate statements or decisions clarified or officially regretted. Even as the dialogue progressed, new problems arose, such as the Carmelite convent at Auschwitz, for which solutions had to be found.

Over the past fifteen years, it has been possible to move forward to new and more open territory and to get a glimpse of exciting possibilities for our future relationship, based on mutual trust, growing friendship, and the realization that Jews and Catholics might finally be able to be, together, a blessing

---

1 Edward Idris Cassidy, *Ecumenism and Interreligious Dialogue: Unitatis redintegratio and Nostra aetate* (New York: Paulist Press, 2005).

to the world. Let me suggest now some aspects of the journey ahead, based on my reading of the past forty years and in particular on my experience over the past fifteen years.

Education

In my opinion, the most important task for the future is not something new. So far we have failed to bring the results of our dialogue adequately to the knowledge of our two communities so that those communities may think and act in conformity with them. While satisfaction is the predominant feeling as the Catholic Church looks back over forty years at *Nostra aetate*, there is certainly urgent work to be done. Jewish speakers often point out that among Catholic clergy, and even among some members of the hierarchy, and consequently among the other members of the Catholic community, *Nostra aetate* and the subsequent radical changes in Catholic-Jewish relations are hardly known, or at least have not been received.

Similarly, I have found in addressing Jewish audiences that many of those present were quite unaware of the same changes. We cannot rest in our implementation of *Nostra aetate* until the anti-Semitism that was more or less taken for granted among Catholics when I was growing up disappears and is replaced by the new spirit of mutual esteem, respect, and friendship.

The need for bringing the fruits of our dialogue into the life of the two communities has been stressed over and over again in the course of our discussions over the years. Cardinal Jan Willebrands was astounded at the beginning of his work in the Commission on Religious Relations with the Jews "to realize how poorly Christians and Jews know each other."[2] Dr. Geoffrey Wigoder of the Institute of Contemporary Jewry of the Hebrew University, Jerusalem, reminded the International Catholic-Jewish Liaison Committee (ILC) at its meeting in Jerusalem in 1994 "of the abyss of ignorance in both our communities concerning the other, which includes dangerous myths and prejudices."[3] The 16th meeting of the ILC in Rome, in March 1998, also discussed "Education: What to do, how to do, and how ought we teach about each other."

In an article published by *The Tablet* on 7 July 2001, Edward Kessler, Executive Director of the Centre for Jewish-Christian Relations in Cambridge, England, agrees that "many of the main divisive issues that have afflicted relations between Christians and Jews have either been eliminated or taken to the furthest point at which agreement is possible." He sees the aim now as getting "these changes into the everyday

---

2   *Information Service* (Pontificium Consilium ad Christianorum Unitatem Fovendam) 17 (1972): 11.

3   A report on this meeting is to be found in *Information Service* (Pontificium Consilium ad Christianorum Unitatem Fovendam) 87 (1994/IV): 231–236, but these words of Dr. Wigoder are from the unpublished working papers of the meeting.

understanding of all the faithful – in the pew and in the *shul*. Critically important are educational guidelines designed for each region."[4] Such education seems all the more necessary in view of the number of new manifestations of anti-Semitism that are reported. The ongoing conflict and violence in the Holy Land between Israel and the Palestinian population has hardened some Catholic hearts once again against the Jewish people, who see such an intimate connection between the land of Israel and their religion.

Efforts are indeed being made within the two communities, and I mention some of them in the hope that they may be multiplied and carried out in more places. Since we are two faith communities, there is a special responsibility here for rabbis and clergy, for if they are not informed then their congregations will probably remain ignorant of what has been done. Some excellent initiatives were undertaken in the nineties both in Canada and in the United States to contact the clergy and seminarians of Central European countries, particularly Poland. In the United States, Canada, and Australia, for example, some Catholic schools are given the opportunity of visiting local synagogues, Jewish schools, and Holocaust museums. Opportunities are provided for students of Catholic and Jewish schools to have time together and so

---

4 Edward Kessler, "The Mission We Can Share," *The Tablet* (7 July 2001): 974–975.

get to know each other. And the invitation for the local rabbi to visit the nearby parish community and for the priest to meet with the synagogue congregation can be a valuable means of education for these communities.

Young people of the present generation have not had the same experience of Catholic-Jewish relations as their predecessors. Younger Catholics, who grew up since Vatican II, may have had little or no personal experience of anti-Semitism. Young Jews will have heard about the horror of the *Shoah*, but they too have been spared the bitter memories of their parents and grandparents. That such a tragedy may never happen again, it seems important that the young people of both communities be brought closer together in a spirit of understanding, mutual esteem, and friendship.

Not long ago, I was invited by the New South Wales Jewish Board of Deputies to launch my latest book at a special commemorative event for the fortieth anniversary of *Nostra aetate*, in the Great synagogue in Sydney. The Governor of New South Wales presided at the event, which was attended by some 400 guests, both Catholic and Jewish. Because the event took place in the first synagogue to be built in Australia, it received good coverage from the media and must surely have been an important teaching lesson for both communities. Whatever means are available to local communities, the task is there and must be undertaken seriously if we wish to eliminate every form of antagonism from within our two communities.

An Unsolved Problem

There is still one question from the past that has not yet been settled to the satisfaction of either side. Already a great deal has been written about Pope Pius XII and the Jewish community during the Second World War. While I was still with the Commission for Religious Relations with the Jews, our efforts to shed more light on the subject failed to do so. The problem was that the Vatican Archives for the period were not open for study, nor indeed were they yet ready for such scientific work.

During the 16th meeting of the ILC in Rome in 1998, this problem was the subject of heated discussion, during which some Jewish participants strongly demanded that the Vatican Archives on the period of Pope Pius XII be opened to accredited Jewish scholars. The CRRJ pointed out that the Vatican had already made available to the public some eleven volumes of documents from the Archives and suggested that, as a first step, Jewish and Catholic scholars together examine this vast source of information about the activities of the Holy See during the Second World War.

A year later, under the auspices of the CRRJ and IJCIC, a group of experts, consisting of three Jewish scholars and the same number of Catholics, was appointed with the mandate to study the eleven volumes of the collection *Actes et Documents du Saint Siège relatifs à la Seconde Guerre Mondiale*. They were asked to report on their work and were given the assurance that, if at the end of their study some questions might need further elucidation from the Archives, attempts would be made to have this done. The experts were never, at any time, led to expect that this meant for them personal access to the documents dated after 1922 in the Vatican Archives.[5] The experts began to meet regularly, and the early signs promised that their study would prove of special value.

After several sessions, the scholars requested a meeting in Rome with the CRRJ. This took place in October 2000. During the meeting the scholars presented a *Preliminary Report*, accompanied by a list of forty-seven questions. Their mandate had not foreseen a *Preliminary Report*, but rather a final report at the end of their study. The situation became more difficult and complicated when the *Preliminary Report* itself was leaked to the press by one of the members and thus became the subject of controversial discussions and public rejection by other scholars.

At the 2001 New York meeting of the ILC, Prof. Michael R. Marrus of the University of Toronto and Rev. Gerard P.

---

5 *Information Service* (Pontificium Consilium ad Christianorum Unitatem Fovendam) 108 (2001/IV): 178.

Fogarty of the University of Virginia, two of the members of the panel, spoke about the work that had been done and expressed their conviction that the *Preliminary Report* makes a valuable contribution to the historical record. The scholars reported that, while differing among themselves, as scholars regularly do, the members of the group were in agreement on the fact that the role of the papacy during the war remains unresolved. Opening the archives, in their opinion, will not definitely put this matter to rest, but it would help to remove the aura of suspicion and contribute to a more mature level of understanding. The ILC took note of the importance of this issue to both communities and encouraged a discourse on the subject that is characterized by mutual respect and appreciation for legitimately held points of view.

Unfortunately, in view of the different interpretations of the group's tasks and aims, coupled with a sentiment of distrust that had been engendered by indiscretions and polemical writings, continued joint study on the question was rendered practically impossible; in July 2001, the scholars suspended their work. In a special statement on the suspension, Cardinal Kasper admitted that the continuation of the study in the circumstances was no longer possible, but he made an important statement for the future:

> Of course, understanding between Jews and Christians also requires an investigation of history. Access to all the relevant historical sources is therefore a natural

prerequisite for this research. The desire of historians to have full access to all the archives concerning the Pontificates of Pius XI (1922–39) and of Pius XII (1939–58) is understandable and legitimate. Out of respect for the truth, the Holy See is prepared to allow access to the Vatican Archives as soon as the work of reorganizing and cataloguing them has been completed.[6]

Cardinal Kasper's promise was followed by the announcement in February 2002 that, even though the cataloguing of all the material between 1922 and 1939 would take about three more years, Pope John Paul II had decided to open to researchers, from the beginning of 2003, the documents in the Archives of the section of the Secretariat of State for Relations with the States and of the Vatican Secret Archives concerning Germany for the period 1922–1939.

The announcement went even further with the promise that once the Vatican Archives for the Pontificate of Pius XI are fully opened, the Vatican will give top priority to making accessible the Vatican-German documentary sources for the Pontificate of Pius XII (1939–1958). While expressing understanding for the fact that historians may well feel frustrated in their research by having access for the present to only one set of documents, the statement expressed the

---

6 *Information Service* (Pontificium Consilium ad Christianorum Unitatem Fovendam) 108 (2001/IV): 178.

hope that this announcement will be "a sound premise for future study and research." The Vatican announced at the same time that it was publishing in two volumes, with the title *Inter Arma Caritas – The Information Office in the Vatican for Prisoners of War instituted by Pius XII (1939–1947)*, the data "concerning prisoners of the last war (1939–1945)" that are preserved in the collection of the Vatican Secret Archives.[7] The dossier containing these documents is complete, homogeneous, and catalogued.[8]

I think the expert group was correct in stating that opening the archives will not definitely put this matter to rest, but will help to remove the aura of suspicion and contribute to a more mature level of understanding. I imagine, however, that historians will still continue well into the future to differ in their judgment on such a delicate and complicated question.

---

7 *Inter arma caritas: l'Ufficio informazioni vaticano per i prigionieri di guerra istituito da Pio XII, 1939–1947*, 2 vols. (Vatican City: Archivio segreto Vaticano, 2004). The two volumes consist of an inventory and documents, 1472 pages in all. In addition, there are eight DVDs that contain the images of the original files in the archive and the names of 2,100,000 prisoners about whom information has been requested.

8 *Vatican Information Service* (9 June 2004): 3.

Questions of Faith

I now offer you a brief glimpse at a new area of development in Jewish-Christian relations that has opened up for us in the past five years, and that I believe shows us new possibilities for the future.

From my earliest days as President of the Holy See's Commission for Religious Relations with the Jews, I have cherished the hope that one day it might be possible for Jewish and Catholic representatives to discuss together questions concerning faith. The first mention I made of this idea was quickly quashed by an Orthodox Jew present at that meeting. Obviously the time had not come for such a discussion, as we had other pressing and serious questions to talk over and problems to solve. Still, I believed that one day we would be able to meet and discuss, as two faith communities, faith questions that are important to both of us.

Within the International Catholic-Jewish Liaison Committee

Within the normal forum for our discussions – the ILC of the Vatican's Commission for Religious Relations with the Jews and the International Jewish Committee for Interreligious Consultation – a particular difficulty in this connection arose from the fact that a number of the Jewish members were not strictly religious Jews. They naturally were concerned solely about the practical questions that engaged us at the time.

For the first time, in 2001, the ILC had a question on its agenda that invited a faith discussion: namely, "Repentance and Reconciliation." Then, the 18th ILC meeting in Buenos Aires in 2004 took as its theme "Justice and Charity: Facing the Challenges of the Future: Jewish and Catholic Relations in the 21st Century."

A *Joint Declaration*[9] published by this meeting must bring renewed hope for further developments in Catholic-Jewish relations. The document begins by acknowledging the "far-reaching changes since the Declaration of the Second Vatican Council *Nostra aetate*," and the special contribution made by Pope John Paul II over the last quarter-century to promoting dialogue between the two faith communities, and "for initiating the fundamental change in Catholic-Jewish relationship." Deliberations on the meeting's theme, "Tzedeq and Tzedaqah" (Justice and Charity), were inspired by God's command to "love one's neighbour as oneself" (Lev 19:18; Mt 22:39). "Drawing from our different perspectives, we have renewed our joint commitment to defend and promote human dignity, as deriving from the biblical affirmation that

---

9   *Information Service* (Pontificium Consilium ad Christianorum Unitatem Fovendam) 116 (2004/III): 139–141.

every human being is created in the likeness and image of God (Gen 1:26)."

The Committee presented this joint commitment to justice as being "deeply rooted in both our faiths," which call on their followers to come to the aid of the needy neighbour. While created in diversity, human beings have the same dignity and every person has "the right to be treated with justice and equality." The *Joint Declaration* states that "Jews and Christians have an equal obligation to work for justice with charity (*Tzedaqah*) which ultimately will lead to Shalom for all humanity. In fidelity to our distinct religious traditions, we see this common commitment to justice and charity as humanity's cooperation in the Divine plan to bring about a better world."

The document recognizes the following as "immediate challenges": the growing economic disparity among people; increasing ecological devastation; the negative aspects of globalization; and the urgent need for international peace-making and reconciliation. There is a strong commitment by both parties to "prevent the re-emergence of antisemitism" and to struggle against terrorism. "Terror, in all its forms, and killing 'in the name of God' can never be justified. Terror is a sin against humanity and God. We call on men and women of all faiths to support international efforts to eradicate this threat to life, so that all nations can live together in peace and security on the basis of *Tzedeq* and *Tzedaqah*."

The importance of this statement is in the fact that a question of common concern, "Justice and Charity," is reflected upon in the light of the two faith traditions. The *Joint Declaration* is also important at this time for the special reference to the fortieth anniversary of *Nostra aetate*. The relative paragraphs merit quotation in full:

> As we approach the 40th anniversary of *Nostra aetate* – the ground-breaking declaration of the Second Vatican Council which repudiated the deicide charge against Jews, reaffirmed the Jewish roots of Christianity and rejected antisemitism – we take note of the many positive changes within the Catholic Church with respect to its relationship with the Jewish People. These past forty years of our fraternal dialogue stand in stark contrast to the almost two millennia of a "teaching of contempt" and all its painful consequences. We draw encouragement from the fruits of our collective strivings which include the recognition of the unique and unbroken relationship between God and the Jewish People and the total rejection of antisemitism in all its forms, including anti-Zionism as a more recent manifestation of antisemitism.
>
> For its part, the Jewish community has evinced a growing willingness to engage in interreligious dialogue and joint action regarding religious, social and communal issues on the local, national, and international levels.... Further, the Jewish community

has made strides in educational programming about Christianity, the elimination of prejudice and the importance of Jewish-Christian dialogue. Additionally, the Jewish community has become more aware of, and deplores, the phenomenon of anti-Catholicism in all its forms, manifesting itself in society at large.

Other Interesting Documents

Certain other documents have appeared in the past five years that I believe can be at once a help and an inspiration for theological discussion between Jews and Catholics.

The year 2000 saw the publication of a document entitled *Dabru Emet: A Jewish Statement on Christians and Christianity*. This is the work of Jewish scholars who wish to make "a thoughtful Jewish response" to what they see as "a dramatic and unprecedented shift in Jewish and Christian relations." They believe that "it is time for Jews to learn about the efforts of Christians to honour Judaism ... and to reflect on what Judaism may now say about Christianity."

Dabru Emet offers eight brief Jewish statements aimed at a better Jewish understanding of Christianity, indicating the basic fact that "Jews and Christians worship the same God ... and seek authority from the same book." Both "respect the moral principles of Torah." The document recognizes that "Nazism was not a Christian phenomenon," but considers that "without the long history of Christian anti-Judaism and Christian violence against Jews, Nazi ideology could not have taken hold nor could it have been carried out."

The authors of this document urge Christians and Jews to work together for justice and peace, and then leave us with a fascinating comment on the "humanly irreconcilable difference between Jews and Christianity," stating that "it will not be settled until God redeems the entire world as promised in the Scripture." By way of explanation, they add: "Each community knows and serves God through their own tradition. Jews can respect Christians' faithfulness to their revelation, just as we expect Christians to respect our faithfulness to our tradition."

Dabru Emet is a remarkable document of particular importance to Catholic-Jewish relations in that any real and lasting advance in Catholic understanding of Jewish teaching will need a corresponding bonding from the Jewish side. As Rabbi Eric Yoffie stated a few months before the publication of *Dabru Emet*, in March 2000, "Catholics need to educate Catholics about Jews, and the Jews to educate Jews about Catholics."[10]

Towards the end of that year, *L'Osservatore Romano* published an article by Cardinal Joseph Ratzinger, then Prefect of

---

10   Eric Yoffie, "Advances and Tensions in Catholic-Jewish Relations: A Way Forward," *Origins* Vol. 29, No. 44 (20 April 2000): 717.

the Congregation for the Doctrine of the Faith, entitled "Abraham's Heritage: A Christmas Gift."[11] While this article was obviously intended to calm the concern that the Jewish community worldwide had expressed with regard to the statement *Dominus Iesus*, of the Congregation for the Doctrine of the Faith, it proved to be a much more significant document, providing further encouragement for Catholic-Jewish theological discussion. Referring to the very negative Jewish reaction to *Dominus Iesus*, "Abraham's Heritage: A Christmas Gift" affirms that "It is evident that, as Christians, our dialogue with the Jews is situated on a different level than that in which we engage with other religions. The faith witnessed to by the Jewish Bible is not merely another religion to us, but is the foundation of our own faith."

Cardinal Ratzinger then gives what has been called "a new vision of the relationship with the Jews." After tracing briefly the history of God's dealings with the Jewish people, the Cardinal expresses "our gratitude to our Jewish brothers and sisters who, despite the hardness of their own history, have held on to faith in this God right up to the present and who witness to it in the sight of those peoples who, lacking

---

11 Reprinted as: "New Vision of the Relationship Between the Church and the Jews," *Origins* Vol. 30, No. 35 (15 February 2001): 565–566.

knowledge of the one God, 'dwell in darkness and the shadow of death' (Lk 1:79)."

The article contains the following interesting comment on relations between Christians and Jews down through the centuries:

> Certainly from the very beginning relations between the infant Church and Israel were often marked by conflict. The Church was considered by its own mother to be a degenerate daughter, while Christians considered their mother to be blind and obstinate. Down through the history of Christianity, already-strained relations deteriorated further, even giving birth in many cases to anti-Jewish attitudes that throughout history have led to deplorable acts of violence. Even if the most recent, loathsome experience of the Shoah was perpetrated in the name of an anti-Christian ideology that tried to strike the Christian faith at its Abrahamic roots in the people of Israel, it cannot be denied that a certain insufficient resistance to this atrocity on the part of Christians can be explained by the inherited anti-Judaism in the hearts of not a few Christians.

For the Cardinal, it is perhaps this latest tragedy that has resulted in a new relationship between the Church and the People of Israel, which he defines as "a sincere willingness to overcome every kind of anti-Judaism and to initiate a constructive dialogue based on knowledge of each other and reconciliation." If such a dialogue is to be fruitful, the Cardinal suggests that "it must begin with a prayer to our God first of all that he might grant to us Christians a greater esteem and love for that people, the people of Israel, to whom belong 'the adoptions as sons, the glory, the covenants, the giving of the law, the worship and the promises; theirs are the patriarchs, and from them, according to the flesh, is the Messiah (Rom 9:4-5),' and this not only in the past, but still today, 'for the gifts and the call of God are irrevocable (Rom 11:29).'" Cardinal Ratzinger goes on to propose to Christians that they in their turn might pray to God "that he grant also to the children of Israel a deeper knowledge of Jesus of Nazareth, who is their son and the gift they have made to us." His final conclusion reminds us of the sixth statement in *Dabru Emet*: "Since we are both waiting the final redemption, let us pray that the paths we follow may converge."

The year 2002 saw the publication of a truly remarkable document entitled *Reflections on Covenant and Mission* by the Ecumenical and Interreligious Affairs Committee of the United States Conference of Catholic Bishops and the National Council of Synagogues USA.[12] The result of discussions between leaders of Jewish and Roman Catholic communities in the United States, who had been meeting twice a year over

---

12 *Reflections on Covenant and Mission* (Washington: United States Conference of Catholic Bishops, 12 August 2002).

a period of two decades, it created great interest among Jews and Catholics involved in dialogue.

For some time it had seemed to many people that the time was ripe for a study on the relationship between the two Covenants that basically describe the nature of the two religious communities and on the consequences of that for Christian mission. The document *Reflections on Covenant and Mission* is an encouraging response that, in the words of the US Bishops' Moderator for Catholic-Jewish Relations, "marks a significant step forward in the dialogue between the Catholic Church and the Jewish community" in the United States.

The Jewish and Catholic reflections are presented separately in the document, but affirm together important conclusions. The Catholic reflections describe the growing respect for the Jewish tradition that has unfolded since the Second Vatican Council. They state:

> A deepening Catholic appreciation of the eternal covenant between God and the Jewish people, together with the divinely-given mission to Jews to witness to God's faithful love, lead to the conclusion that campaigns that target Jews for conversion to Christianity are no longer theologically acceptable in the Catholic Church.

The document stresses that evangelization, or mission, as the Church's work cannot be separated from its faith in Jesus Christ, in whom Christians find the kingdom present and fulfilled. But it points out that this evangelizing mission goes far beyond "the invitation to a commitment to faith in Jesus Christ and to entry through baptism into the community of believers that is the Church. It includes the Church's activities of presence and witness; commitment to social development and human liberation; Christian worship, prayer, and contemplation; interreligious dialogue; and proclamation and catechesis."

But given the "utterly unique relationship of Christianity with Judaism" and the many aspects of this spiritual linkage, "the Catholic Church has come to recognize that its mission of preparing for the coming of the kingdom is one that is shared with the Jewish people, even if Jews do not conceive of this task Christologically as the Church does." In view of this, the document quotes Prof. Tommaso Federici and Cardinal Walter Kasper to state that there should not be in the Church any organization dedicated to the conversion of the Jews. From the Catholic point of view, Judaism is a religion that springs from divine revelation. Cardinal Kasper states:

> God's grace, which is the grace of Jesus Christ according to our faith, is available to all. Therefore, the Church believes that Judaism, i.e. the faithful response of the Jewish people to God's irrevocable covenant, is salvific for them, because God is faithful to his promises.

Since, in Catholic teaching, both the Church and the Jewish people abide in Covenant with God, they both therefore have missions before God to undertake in the world. The Church believes that the mission of the Jewish people is not restricted to their historical role as the people from whom Jesus was born "according to the flesh" (Rom 9:5) and from whom the Church's apostles came. It quotes the following statement from Cardinal Ratzinger: "God's providence ... has obviously given Israel a particular mission in this time of the Gentiles." Only the Jewish people themselves can articulate their mission, "in the light of their own religious experience." The Catholic section of the document concludes with this profound statement:

> With the Jewish people, the Catholic Church, in the words of *Nostra aetate*, "awaits the day, known to God alone, when all peoples will call on God with one voice and serve him shoulder to shoulder."

The Jewish reflections are given the title "The Mission of the Jews and the Perfection of the World." This mission is described as threefold, as rooted in Scripture and developed in later Jewish sources:

> There is, first, the mission of covenant – the ever-formative impetus to Jewish life that results from the covenant between God and the Jews. Second, there is the mission of witness, whereby the Jews see themselves "and are frequently seen by others" as God's

eternal witnesses to His existence and to his redeeming power in the world. And third, there is the mission of humanity, a mission that understands the Biblical history of the Jews as containing a message to more than the Jews alone. It presupposes a message and a mission addressed to all human beings.

The document describes the mission of Covenant and witness, before dealing at greater length with the mission of humanity. It states that the message of the Bible is a message and a vision not only to Israel but to all of humanity. It then reminds the reader that Isaiah speaks twice of the Jews as a light to peoples and quotes the experience of Jonah to illustrate that it is a mistake to think that God is concerned only with the Jews:

> The God of the Bible is the God of the world. His visions are visions for all of humanity. His love is a love that extends to every creature ... Adam and Eve were His first creations and they are created long before the first Jews. They are created in the image of God, as are all of their children to eternity. Only the human creation is in the divine image. *Tikun ha-olam,* that is, perfection or repairing of the world, is a joint task of the Jews and all humanity. Though Jews see themselves as living in a world that is as yet unredeemed, God wills His creatures to participate in the world's repair.

Finally, the Jewish reflections point out certain practical conclusions that follow from the threefold "mission" in classical Judaism, and that suggest a joint agenda for Christians and Jews. The reflection begins with the following statement:

> Although Christians and Jews understand the messianic hope involved in that perfection quite differently, still, whether we are waiting for the messiah – as Jews believe – or for the Messiah's second coming – as Christians believe – we share the belief that we live in an unredeemed world that longs for repair.

Then it asks: "Why not articulate a common agenda? Why not join together our spiritual forces to state and to act upon the values we share in common and that lead to the repair of the unredeemed world?" Looking then to the Talmud, the document draws from that source thoughts about repairing the world, giving details of charity directed to the poor and deeds of kindness to all, the poor and the rich, the living and the dead; creating an economy where people are encouraged to help one another financially as an expression of their common fellowship; fulfilling our obligations to the sick and mourners; and preserving the dignity of the aged. While Jewish law is of course directed at Jews, and its primary concern is to encourage the expression of love to the members of the community, it points out that many of these actions are mandatory towards all people, and quotes the Talmud as saying:

One must provide for the needs of the gentile poor with the Jewish poor. One must visit the gentile sick with the Jewish sick. One must care for the burial of a gentile, just as one must care for the burial of a Jew. [These obligations are universal] because these are the ways of peace.

Not everyone in the two communities will agree with all that is stated in this document. In fact, when these *Reflections* were published, they created a wide-ranging dispute within the Roman Catholic Church in the United States, but also in wider ecumenical and interfaith circles. Most of the argument centred on the question of whether Christians should desire and pray for the conversion of Jews. There was no question in this discussion of Church organizations aiming to convert Jews, but leading Church officials expressed the view that it would be absurd to think that the mission given to the Church by Christ is only for pagans and not for Jews, when all of Christ's preaching and his call to conversion was addressed precisely to the Jews. At the same time, Pope John Paul II, on a number of occasions, made it clear that the first Covenant has not been revoked and that therefore the Church is called to concentrate on its mission "with" the Jews, rather than "to" the Jews.[13] The national Jewish-Catholic dialogue in the

---

13 "Should Christians still seek to convert Jews?" *The Tablet* (12 July 2003), 13.

United States has certainly posed a challenge that can and should be addressed by Christians and Jews.

Dialogue with the Chief Rabbinate of Israel

In conclusion, I wish to bring to your attention a most significant event related to possible theological discussions between Catholics and Jews: namely, a dialogue between a special Catholic committee appointed by the Vatican and the Great Rabbinate of Israel. This was certainly made possible by the visit to Israel in 2000 of Pope John Paul II, who on that occasion spent quite some time at the Chief Rabbinate in discussion with the two Chief Rabbis of Israel. This event also offered members of the Pope's entourage and a number of Jewish rabbis the possibility of coming to know one another. Cardinal Kasper followed up these promising contacts with a personal visit to Israel in November 2001.

After a preliminary meeting in Jerusalem on 5 June 2002, high-ranking delegations from both sides met in Villa Cavalletti, Grottaferrata, in the vicinity of Rome from 23–27 February 2003. The Jewish delegation was led by the Chief Rabbi of Haifa, Shar Yishuv Cohen; the Catholic delegation was led by Cardinal Jorge Mejia, a former Secretary of the CRRJ. The meeting was conducted in a warm and friendly atmosphere of mutual goodwill and was characterized by the effort to highlight common aspects of both traditions. Two main issues were raised: "The Sanctity of Life" and "The Value of the Family."

A *Common Declaration*[14] was signed at the end of the meeting, in which the two delegations rejected any attempt to destroy human life, based on their common religious understanding that the human being is created in the image of God. Every human life is "holy, sacrosanct and inviolable." They stated clearly that it is a profanation of religion to declare oneself a terrorist in the name of God or to do violence to others in God's name. They emphasized the need that both communities have, particularly for the younger generation, for education in respect of the holiness of human life, and agreed that "against the present trend of violence and death in our societies, we should foster our cooperation with believers of all religions and all people of goodwill in promoting a culture of life."

The participants at this gathering also insisted on the institution of the family as stemming from the will of the Almighty. They declared that "Marriage in a religious perspective has a great value, because God blessed this union and sanctified it.... The family unit is the basis for a wholesome society."

This meeting was a historical breakthrough, since until then it had not been possible to organize an official dialogue

---

14 *Information Service* (Pontificium Consilium ad Christianorum Unitatem Fovendam) 112 (2003/I): 35–36.

between the CRRJ and Institutes in Israel. Moreover, for the first time the Church was able to enter into dialogue with all the different forms of Judaism: Orthodox, Conservative, and Reformed.

A second meeting between the Chief Rabbinate of Israel and the CRRJ took place in Jerusalem on 1–3 December 2003 to discuss the theme "The Relevance of Central Teachings in the Holy Scriptures Which We Share for Contemporary Society and the Education of Future Generations." The *Joint Declaration*[15] issued on this occasion noted that once again the deliberations had taken place in an atmosphere of mutual respect and amity, and that satisfaction was expressed "regarding the firm foundations that have already been established between the two delegations with great promise for continuity and effective collaboration."

The participants in this second formal meeting continued their reflections on the relation of the family to the Scriptures and declared that "humankind is one family with moral responsibility for one another." They saw that "awareness of this reality leads to the religious and moral duty that may serve as a true charter for human rights and dignity in our modern world and provide a genuine vision for a just society, universal peace and well-being." It was emphasized that "the response to the challenge of promoting religious faith in

---

15   Ibid., 114 (2003/IV): 200.

contemporary society requires us to provide living examples of justice, loving kindness, tolerance and humility," as set forth in the Scriptures.

The meeting stressed the need for religious education to provide hope and direction for positive living in human solidarity and harmony in our complex modern society. The participants called on religious leaders and educators to instruct their communities to pursue the paths of peace and well-being of society at large. A special appeal was addressed to the family of Abraham and a call made to all believers "to put aside weapons of war and destruction – 'to seek peace and pursue it' (Ps 34:15)."

A further meeting was held in Jerusalem on 26–28 June 2005, having as its theme "The Relationship between Religious and Civil Authority in the Jewish and Christian Traditions," based on the biblical vision of the distinct roles of Priest, Prophet, and King, as well as their respective relationships with the People of God.

The following key points were made:[16]

1. Religious values are crucial for the well being of the individual and society.
2. The purpose of civil authority is to serve and provide for the welfare of the people through respecting the life and dignity of every individual.

---

16 Ibid., 119 (2005/III): 145.

3. While emphasising the importance of democracy in this regard, at the same time it is essential to legally protect society from extreme individualism, exploitation by vested interest groups and insensitivity to the cultural and moral values of religious tradition.

4. Freedom of religion must be guaranteed to both individuals and communities by the religious and civil authorities.

5. The relationship between religion and state must be based on reciprocity, mutual respect and cooperation.

6. Legislation for the promotion of particular religious values is legitimate when done in harmony with the principles of human rights.

7. We have an ethical obligation to demonstrate religious responsibility in these regards, and especially to educate future generations through engaging media opinion-makers as well as through conventional educational channels.

Discussion followed on the responsibility of the State to guarantee the rights of all religious communities, giving special attention to the situation and needs of the Christian communities in the Holy Land, as well as to the needs of the Jewish communities around the world, facilitating full social and political equality without undermining particular identities.

Conclusion

I believe that we can see in all these recent developments a way forward in Christian-Jewish relations. In a message to a special event in Rome to commemorate the fortieth anniversary of *Nostra aetate*,[17] Pope Benedict XVI wrote that dialogue between Jews and Christians "must continue to enrich and deepen the bonds of friendship which have developed, while preaching and catechesis must be committed to ensuring that our mutual relations are presented in the light of the principles set forth by the Council."

His Holiness expressed the hope that

> both in theological dialogue and in everyday contacts and collaboration, Christians and Jews will offer an ever more compelling shared witness to the One God and His commandments, the sanctity of life, the promotion of human dignity, the rights of the family and the need to build a world of justice, reconciliation and peace for future generations.

This seems to sum up well the future challenge: a shared commitment to healing a broken world.

---

17   *Vatican Information Service*, 28 October 2005.

5

ISSUES FACING CHRISTIAN-JEWISH DIALOGUE

Rabbi Riccardo Di Segni
Chief Rabbi of Rome

The discussion of the relationship between Christianity and Judaism has particular symbolic significance for me, a representative of the Jewish community in Rome. This community, in fact, represents the oldest Jewish settlement in the West, remaining stable, without interruption, for over twenty-one centuries. The Jews preceded the arrival of the Christians – who at the beginning were themselves Jews – by almost two centuries and succeeded in staying in Rome, the heart of Christianity, thanks to or despite their relationship with the Church's authority – so close and so distant from them. Still today, other than the important and clamorous public encounters of representatives from the two faith communities, interactions occur on a daily basis, primarily in the relations of everyday people. A visitor who exits the Vatican will often encounter, among the people outside the walls, a street vendor who is a Roman Jew.

It is timely to evaluate the importance of the document *Nostra aetate*, for today and for the future, forty years after its promulgation. This document represents, in the history of the Church and its relations with Judaism, an epochal event and an essential point of reference. Since the time of the document's promulgation, the Church has never been the same. Progress in terms of respect and mutual debate has been, without a doubt, significant. One might be tempted to speak about *Nostra aetate* and its effects on dialogue between Jews and Christians since Vatican II in substantially praising terms. However, one should proceed with a certain degree of caution or critical attention. Many problems are still unresolved, perhaps because *Nostra aetate* was not able to resolve them or even because it did not want to resolve them.

One of the main problems surrounds the ultimate intent of the dialogue between the two faiths. Alongside this problem are a series of single episodes and a few doctrinal statements. It is important to understand the two worlds of Judaism and Catholicism forty years ago, at the time when they were comparing their positions. For the Jews, at least in the beginning, the priority was for Catholics to end disrespectful preaching and denounce anti-Jewish hostility present at the heart of Christian doctrine. Regarding this issue, at least from the doctrinal point of view, the approach of *Nostra aetate* was noteworthy. There was also some discussion of the Holocaust. Even though the Jewish world was not satisfied that Catholics had taken their share of responsibility for it, at least the document represented a point of departure for a future of living together in a non-aggressive manner. Once this key point was resolved, or at least addressed, the issues regarding theology were opened. The Jewish position, in dialogue with the Christians, was centred on one key point: we speak for the purpose of getting to know each other, not for the purpose of conversion. Judaism is not interested in the conversion – in the sense of changing one's religion – of its non-Jewish dialogue partner. A Christian who debates with a Jew can be sure of the fact that the Jew will not try to convert him or her. At most, and only in extreme cases, the Jew might question the Christian on theological matters related to his or her monotheistic outlook. All of this is quite different for the Christian, who historically bases his faith on a duty to evangelize, and considers Judaism the origin of his faith, albeit an incomplete one in need of perfection.

In the course of Christianity's long history, the intent to convert was one of the poisons that most infected its relations with Judaism. One could have hoped that the new climate over the last forty years would have cleansed this poison. However, this has not been the case. Indeed, Jews and Catholics have done a great deal to impede the continuation of anti-Jewish behaviour, but Catholics have still not renounced the principle of converting Jews as an ideal. One action that confirms this position was the long process that brought Edith Stein first to beatification and then later to sainthood. Edith Stein was born into a Jewish family and later converted to Catholicism after completing important philosophical studies at university. She joined a German convent and became a nun. When the Nazis arrived she fled to a Dutch convent. There, she was captured and sent to Auschwitz, where she met her death in a gas chamber. A monumental process brought her to greater glory, making her a patron saint of Europe.

The Jewish world did not like this. Actually, it viewed this process as alarming because the Church had underlined Edith Stein's spiritual path as an ideal Jewish path. Pope John Paul II referred to her as a "new Esther." It is forgotten that in her times, anyone who converted from Judaism had to make an oath promising to abandon "Jewish superstition." The tragic death of Stein, about which there is obviously a respectful silence on the part of the Jews, was accompanied by evidence that attributed to Stein the declaration in which she offers a sacrifice for the sins of her Jewish brothers and sisters, guilty for the consistent failure to recognize the divinity of Jesus. Whether this is true or not, the fact is that the Church's recent hagiography has accepted it. In our opinion, this results in offering a monstrous interpretation of the meaning of the

Holocaust and is a further source of aggravation in a process where the message is that the saintly Jew is the one who converts to Christianity.

This episode is not an isolated one, and the list of painful examples on this topic could be long: from the tones used in the recent polemic about the conversions of children in post-war France; to the use – which the Jewish side considers, at the least, indelicate – of converted Jews who have reached prominent positions in the Church and who act ostentatiously during debates or negotiations; to the case of the ninety-year-old Florentine Jew, sick and not very mentally lucid, who was converted by a zealous priest in the Jewish nursing home with the protection of the archbishop of his city, who responded to the protests by stating that he will forewarn the Jewish community in the event of any other future cases.

Aside from these facts, which could be relegated to the margins with a certain degree of benevolence, there still exists the problem of a theology that has a hard time examining itself when it comes to its exceptional relations with Judaism. In the writings of the former Cardinal Joseph Ratzinger, a constant theme emerges: along with profound respect for its Jewish roots, there is a sense that the dialogue is a missionary instrument, an invitation to Judaism to consider Jesus as the Messiah.

Perhaps, though, it is in the same words of the former Cardinal Ratzinger that we can find a way out of this theological impasse, which threatens to prejudice the future of our relations. The Cardinal spoke repeatedly about the noble exercise of patience in regards to our lack of knowledge of the divine plan. Might we distinguish between hopes fed by the doctrine and the political behaviour of the twisting of these problems in an eschatological perspective? If we speak of *eschaton*, i.e. the end of time, we can get along, but if our patience is more limited in time, then we have problems. In what way does the dialogue between Catholics and Jews allow for the peaceful, private, and fundamental declaration of faith of everyone?

If one could sum up the state of relations forty years after *Nostra aetate*, one could say that respect has grown noticeably, but trust has not grown between the two religions. The era of suspicion is not over. In summer 2005, during evening prayer, Pope Benedict XVI quoted a comment by Augustine, which states: "We are the Israel of God and … we are Israel: the Israel on which is peace." This suggests once again that Christianity replaces the original Judaism. This is precisely what *Nostra aetate* did not resolve. It claimed that "The Church is the new people of God…." There has been substantial progress from the expression "True Israel" (meaning the only one, while the other is false) to "New Israel," but there is no explanation about if and how the "New" entirely or in part substitutes the "Old." As far as the name for the Jewish people is concerned, in official documents one can note a certain resistance to calling them the "people of Israel." Perhaps this is due to political considerations (to avoid confusion with the State of Israel), but for the reason just mentioned it is of a non-friendly, problematic nature.[1]

The relationship between Judaism and Christianity is complex and problematic. It requires from both sides infinite patience and a willingness to listen and exchange ideas. I believe that even with all the difficulties, the Church has proven it listens and that it is willing to exchange ideas, even if the times and methods have not been ideal.

The roads that brought Judaism and Christianity to the need for constructive confrontation after almost 2,000 years of hostility were different, like every other thing that pertained to the history of these two worlds. We are using *Nostra aetate* as a point of reference, but the process was born much earlier. From at least the age of the Enlightenment, when the Church had difficulty examining itself and accepting new liberal ideas, it opposed the winds of revolution. In defending its tradition, it stuck with obstinate loyalty to its classical model of relations with the Jews, bringing forward, often with incredible harshness and at other times with paternalism, a substantial hostility with regards to Judaism. The Church's acceptance

---

[1] One should note, however, an important variation of this tendency (in the speech addressed to me) in Pope Benedict XVI's papal audience on January 17, 2006, in which there was an unequivocal definition of the Jews as people of Israel.

of modernity and of democratic principles, together with expressing its horror towards the Holocaust, produced the beginning of an epochal transformation. The path of Judaism was different. In the last two centuries, it met with the contradictions and illusions of civic equality offered and accepted with enthusiasm, the rebirth of a national political entity, and the most horrible mass persecution in its history. In all these events the Church (the churches) appeared for the most part as the usual out-of-touch and hostile power with whom it would not have made sense to enter into dialogue, except to tell it to lessen its harsh tones. The proposal for dialogue with Christians came almost by surprise. Often Judaism was regarded as an invited party in this dialogue. And the invitation was responded to in various ways – from refusal, to acceptance out of necessity, to even enthusiasm – and each time, with founded reasons. But this past perspective must be re-examined.

For Judaism these are new times, unimaginable just fifty or sixty years ago. From the ashes of the Holocaust rose a state in which half the world's Jews will soon live. In every place in the Western world, the rapport with the Jews has changed radically. All this cannot leave Judaism indifferent and make it reason with the same conditions of a painful past. It requires a re-evaluation of Judaism's role in relation to other peoples and religions of the world. First and foremost, it requires a re-evaluation of Judaism's relationship towards those, like Christians, who in many ways are closest to us.

We have perhaps overcome the difficulties of the initial phases of the dialogue. We have gained experience, overcome some problems, and encountered new ones or put them aside because they are considered less urgent. We must move forward in ways and with plans yet to be invented for our own good and for the good of everyone, because the existential questions posed to us by this very new moment in history cannot remain unanswered.

6
FINDING A PLACE FOR THE OTHER: CHALLENGES FACING THE FUTURE OF JEWISH-CHRISTIAN DIALOGUE

James F. Puglisi, SA
Minister General, Franciscan Friars of the Atonement

Although I am not a specialist in the question of Jewish-Christian relations, as is Cardinal Cassidy or Rabbi Di Segni, I am concerned with the dynamics of dialogue itself. I realize the importance of this dialogue for other dialogues between Christian churches and between Christians and peoples of other living faiths.

I would like to divide my reflections into several sections. I begin with some personal observations explaining my particular starting point. This serves to set the scene for what I feel is a very important method in the dialogue process. Second, I consider dialogue as a journey – not just any journey, but a particular one, namely a "learning journey." Next, I offer some thoughts on a stance that has worked well in other dialogues:

the healing of memories. Fourth, I examine the results of this healing: a process going from repentance to conversion and ending with pardon. Finally, I offer some conclusions dealing with the impact and fulfillment of *Nostra aetate*.

A Place for the Other

I am a Franciscan Friar of the Atonement. Being Franciscan puts me in direct relationship to the heart of what I feel needs to be a central theme, if not the central theme: "a place for the other." "Finding a place for the other" is what defines the understanding of the Franciscan vocation as Francis of Assisi received it from God. His call was to live a life of "minority," of being a "lesser brother." What this means is that Francis and his followers practised a life of self-effacement, or *kenosis*, or "emptying out" so that the Other might find a dwelling place. Of course this is really not a new intuition, since the Bible is filled with men and women who sought to do this, to live authentically the Covenant that *Adonai* had made with the people. The extent to which they could make room for the stranger in their lives was a sign of the extent to which they could welcome (*hesed*) the Lord into their lives. The understanding of minority in the Franciscan tradition is very much linked to the understanding of welcoming the stranger into one's home, into one's life. Hence the sense of hospitality that is found in all of our Friaries or homes, which should be a hallmark of true human existence and therefore of divine presence.

The authorized biography of Francis of Assisi by Bonaventure of Bagnoregio[1] illustrates wonderfully how Francis of Assisi, without understanding fully what was happening to himself, progressively, and not without many failures, was creating space within himself for his Creator and assuming a new identity which was not self-referencing but rather was defined in terms of the Other. The question he continually asked was, "Who are you, O Lord, that I may know who I am?" As long as he was filled with himself, he could not even begin to ask this question. Slowly, however, he found that he was at odds with himself, never content or satisfied, and always restless until he found that *shalom* (not peace but integrity, unity) in the Other and the Other in him. This was done by creating space for others in his life by a sense of service to others – in fact, by seeing himself and his brothers as lesser brothers, as servants of all.

The process of creating space for the Other is not really a psychological process, but a theological and spiritual one. In my eyes, the difficulty we have had in connecting with one another in the past is that both partners in this "dialogue" have not engaged in this theological and spiritual process. It seems

---

1 Bonaventure of Bagnoregio, *Bonaventure: The Soul's Journey into God; The Tree of Life; The Life of St. Francis*, trans. Ewert Cousins (New York: Paulist Press, 1978).

to me that what we have been engaged in is more a negotiation than a dialogue. The example of Francis of Assisi is obviously not based on a negotiation with God, with neighbour – in short, with the Other – but rather a dialogue, an exchange of gifts, learning about oneself through the other. This way of learning is consistent with what we know anthropologically about our identity. No one can appropriate their identity by themselves. Rather, their identity is in a certain way given to them. In other words, there is an exchange of communication, of information about one's self, which must be assimilated into the identity. The identity is not self-referencing. If this was the case, then the person would have been made in the "image and likeness of oneself" rather than in the image and likeness of God, the Other, and mediated through the encounters with others. If we are to find a place for the Other, then we will need to create that space, which ultimately means giving up some of our own space. We will return to this point in a moment.

Dialogue as a "Learning Journey"

Many trips have been taken to visit the concentration camps by groups of Jews and Christians together. This journey may be described as a "learning journey." Learning because we are both unlearning some things about the other and at the same time learning, or maybe relearning, some things that were either new or had been forgotten. At the heart of this journey remains the horrific experience of the *Shoah*.

For many decades in the last century, the experience of the Holocaust was like an ominous black shadow hovering over the generations of men and women who were its survivors, who were its living memory. For other persons, it was a historical event that had been sanitized and, unfortunately in some cases, rationalized by theories, which by any standard today would be labelled as insane, demonic, or evil. When I was in high school and we studied the Nazi regime, we watched films of the suppression of human life in the camps. The horrific scenes were shocking for the spirits of young teenagers and provoked a serious debate among educators about the use of such footage at the high school level. But here is where the first learning or unlearning began. Although the majority of the students were Christian, it was a public school, so it was not in a religious context that we began to learn about humanity's inhumanity. Obviously, the memory of the Holocaust was kept alive in the Jewish household in a different way and from a different perspective. It is unfortunate that there was no exchange in the way the historical event was presented between the two communities. Each told the history as they saw it and from their perspective. In the recounting of this history, often times there was no place for the Other, because it was about "me" and not the Other.

As Cardinal Cassidy has pointed out it, was only towards the end of the last century that a learning journey began to happen. I call this a journey because it was a displacing from one place to another, both in the physical sense as well as in the spiritual and anthropological senses. It is still too early to describe this process as a dialogue, because in many respects there was not yet an exchange between two partners or persons; only one side of the experience was being represented. It was only gradually that both sides or partners began to realize that the memory of the *Shoah* had other details, other actors, who had had the same experience. We must be careful not to affirm that the experience was the same for both partners, since this would amount to a distortion of the reality and of the truth of what happened; rather, we must realize that there was a solidarity in the sin of what happened, even though the perception of what happened is different.

I would like to look at this unique instance as an example of how far we have both come in learning more about what happened, to whom, by whom, with what result, and how there is a gradual awareness that it is not just "all about me": "others" can relate to what happened because they share the same memory of the event. I believe this is what Cardinal Keeler was referring to when he described the experience of a Catholic-Jewish pilgrimage to Auschwitz in 1992. What the experience of dialogue as a learning journey proves is that no one person or group possesses the whole of the experience or the memory. What is essential in this dialogue is that each is allowed to share their part of the memory of the story and in turn allows it to be completed by the other. Together, and only then, will we have the whole story as part of our collective memory.

Moreover, this learning journey will also make room for the pain of the past. It will create a space for forgiveness. It will require reconciliation in the sense of finding *shalom* again in our relationships. This type of dialogue in the future will not be based on negotiation. Rather, it will be constructed on the basis of a regained mutual respect that has indeed created space for the other in terms of existence, thereby forming a whole, an integral reality, composed of diverse parts. For this to happen, there is an urgent need for a healing (not cancellation) of memories.

Healing of Memories

Far too often, we return to some stumbling block raised from the dark of our past, our historical memories. It may be useful to refer here to some reflections of the French philosopher Paul Ricœur. He has offered some very intriguing ideas in an essay prepared for the European parliament in the whole process of the unity of Europe. He speaks of the need to reach the very memory of humanity and seek its healing.² In the context of the future of Europe, he raises the point of the inability of peoples to go beyond their past. Needless to say, he does not propose that we forget or cancel our past; this would be irresponsible, since we always learn from our past. However, the dangerous hurts that reside in our memories need to be somehow healed. In the Judeo-Christian tradition, we cannot give up our memories, since it is in these that we encounter God. But how do we encounter God there except in and through our own proper histories? This is precisely where the problem arises. When we recount, or retell, our histories, we often do so with selective memories. We tell the things that we want to emphasize or that will support our points of view or even put us in a more favourable light. What is established is a "narrative identity" of those involved in the story. In this way, it becomes easy to vilify one or the other depending on who is telling the story. The sequence of events can be reordered and thereby given a different twist or spin by the one who recounts the story. This effect is referred to as a "mobile identity." What happens, then, is that "the narrative identity participates in the mobility of the recounting and in its dialectic of order and disorder."³ This is what we do when

---

2 Paul Ricœur, "Quel éthos nouveau pour l'Europe?" in *Imaginer l'Europe. Le marché intérieur européen, tâche culturelle et économique*, ed. P. Koslowski (Paris: Cerf, 1992), 107–116.

3 Ibid., 110.

we tell the history of others and why we have several versions of the same event retold. Ricœur explains:

> If each one receives a certain narrative identity from the histories which are told of them or that they tell of themselves, this identity is mixed with that of others in such a way as to engender stories on a second level which are themselves the intersections between several stories.[4]

To put it another way, every history of an individual or of a religion is at the same time a segment of the history of the life of another. In the context of the reconciliation or exchange of memories, the history of the other needs to be translated with imagination and sympathy. The mobile identifications contribute to the reconfiguration of our own past and of the past of others through a constant remodelling of the histories we tell about ourselves and about others.[5] One of the first steps of a dialogue is to begin to retell our stories together. In this process, words alone will be insufficient: it is not by composing "new histories" that the wounds of the past will be healed and the corrections of misperceptions righted, but rather by the pardon that will be granted. This is perhaps the most powerful aspect of this "putting into practice." Ricœur sees the importance of tradition at this juncture. What he

---

4 Ibid.
5 Ibid.

understands by tradition is "transmission, transmission of things said, of beliefs professed, of norms assumed, and so forth. However, such a transmission is only lively if tradition remains the other partner of the pair which it forms with innovation."[6] This innovation is the indispensable part of the dynamic liberating the future from tradition. We cannot simply repeat what we have received (lest we betray what we have received). We must constantly reinterpret what we have received for our generation and for the next. This is the way in which tradition becomes intelligible.

Another element necessary in this process is the need to embark on acts of repentance (*teshuva*), leading to pardon or forgiveness.

Repentance, Conversion, Pardon

The healing of memories passes through a process that ends in pardon. Ricœur treats a model of pardon as something central to the healing of memories. At the heart of the Covenant made with Israel is the offer of pardon. At the heart of the Gospel is the call to forgiveness. Starting from this perspective, Ricœur understands the model of pardon as a new way of revising the past, and through it, the narrative identity of each one. Seeing these personal histories, stories,

---

6   Ibid., 112.

pasts being intertwined is likewise a way of seeing that these histories, stories, pasts must be told together. This is where we can see the results of the exchange, or the healing of memories, taking place. Ricœur says that "pardon is likewise a specific form of this mutual revision from which deliverance of promises not kept in the past is a very precious effect."[7] What I am suggesting here does not mean cancelling the past but rather going beyond those things that tend to perpetuate a state of alienation (and hence do not create a space for the Other). In this sense, we may talk about changing our common future.

In Ricœur's words,

> The exchange of memories required by our ... model, demands, according to this new model [of pardon], the exchange of the memory of suffering inflicted and experienced. Now this exchange requires more than the imagination and sympathy that I evoked above. More than anything else, it has something to do with pardon, to the degree that pardon consists in *"releasing the debt."*

He continues,

> The 'poetic' power [of pardon] consists in the releasing or breaking of the law of irreversibility of time, changing, if not, the past as a collection of things that

---

7   Ibid., 113.

happened, at least its meaning for men and women of the present. It does this by removing the weight of the guilt which paralyzes the relationship of men acting and suffering in their own history. It does not *abolish* the debt since we are and remain the inheritors of the past but it removes the suffering of the debt.[8]

In his reflections at the fourth European day of Jewish culture, Cardinal Walter Kasper noted that

> especially with regard to antisemitism and to the *Shoah*, we can justifiably speak of the need to embark on acts of repentance (*teshuva*), resulting in exemplary and concrete acts which, "as members of the Church, we are linked to the sins as well as the merits of all her children" (*We Remember: A Reflection on the Shoah*, n. V). This is how we need to interpret Pope John Paul II's gestures made both on 12 March 2000 and confirmed on 26 March in Jerusalem at the Western or Wailing Wall of the Temple.[9]

A recent example of this point among Christians was the return to the Patriarch of Constantinople of the relics of two of the most important holy men for the Orthodox. This gesture did not erase the past, but it enabled us to tell the story of how these precious objects arrived where they did.

---

8   Ibid.

9   Walter Kasper, "Antisemitism: A Wound to Be Healed" *L'Osservatore Romano*, English Edition 40 (10 January 2003): 6.

It was a moment of confronting our Western history with the Orthodox, enabling each side to retell their recollection of events and to verify where the truth lay in relation to this page of their common history. This act was possible only after years of difficult dialogue, which allowed for the opening of a space for the other, be it ever so small. This historical event symbolized the possibility of both dialogue partners being true to their memory without falsifying the memory of the other. This is one of the central issues of the type of theological dialogue that we need between Jews and Christians, where we ask the question "How can I be true to my own faith without being false to yours?"

Conclusion: The Impact and Fulfillment of *Nostra aetate*

Perhaps one of the most important achievements of the Declaration *Nostra aetate* was that it helped Christians realize that, to be fully Christian, we need to fully understand Judaism. In order for this to happen, many misconceptions and misrepresentations of Judaism needed to be removed or purified. One of the most serious misrepresentations of the Jewish people erroneously portrayed Jews as unfaithful, holding them collectively responsible for the death of Jesus. A serious effort has been made by Catholics since the Second Vatican Council to correct these misconceptions, to revise the teaching about Judaism and the Jewish people, and to articulate more clearly a theology that proclaims the unique bond that exists between Christianity and Judaism. The result of such an effort is a deepening of our own Christian faith.

In this effort I believe that Catholic Christians are coming to a more accurate appreciation of Jews and Judaism. Several points may illustrate this understanding.

First is the relationship of the Jewish people to the Covenant of God. The enduring validity of the Covenant made with Israel is fully accepted within Catholic theology. It has, however, been a long and arduous journey whereby a theology of supersessionism has been repudiated. Nevertheless, residue remains in the minds of some. Perhaps the most important element that will help us to fully purify our theology and practice of this tendency is to recognize the vibrant, living faith being practised by our Jewish brothers and sisters.

Second, in the Catholic practice of worship today, thanks to the cultic practice of Jews, we have come to centre more our prayer life and worship on the one God, due to the example of Jesus, who was fully observant in his practice of Judaism. To understand his teaching, his actions, his life we need to understand Judaism in its teachings, actions, and ethos. Perhaps we have difficulty here because of the complexities of the various traditions within Judaism. No doubt this same phenomenon within Christianity confuses Jews trying to understand the diverse traditions and ways of expressing the

Christian faith. In this, then, we have a common experience in which we may share as part of our dialogue.

Third, to many Christians, Judaism appears as a tangle of complex laws and prescriptions. Some Christians express what they see as legalistic or even ritualistic. However, this rich and long interpretive tradition demonstrates the living organic nature of Judaism in its attempt to enrich its life, faith, and self-understanding. Moreover, this literary tradition is not always accessible to Christians: hence, a space opens for developing an erroneous understanding of contemporary Judaism.

Fourth, at times it is difficult to know and to appreciate Judaism because there seem to be spokespeople or organizations who speak on behalf of Jews, rather than representatives of living Judaism. These may be perceived as groups of a political nature who are negotiating objectives rather than entering into dialogue. It is often confusing to know who represents "official" Judaism and the various traditions within Judaism. For Catholics, it is clear who are the "official" spokespersons: the bishops and, ultimately, the pope in communion with the bishops. The various organizations in the Jewish world may seem to function as lobby groups. The result does not cast a positive light on the vitality of Judaism.

Fifth is the Bible. In my experience, some Jews have a much better understanding of the Christian scriptures than do Christians, because Jews read the writings of Jesus and the disciples through Jewish eyes. Christians often forget that these men and women of the first generation were Jews: living, practising Jews. Christian interpretations of Jesus' sayings may often be superficial and miss the point. They read the text without knowing the Semitic roots of the teaching and its connection to the Hebrew Scriptures.

Sixth is the mission of Judaism. What do Jews see as their mission in the modern world? How is this historically related to Israel's vocation in relation to the Covenant, and how is it to be carried out? A related question is this: Is there any space for Christianity in this mission today? I think these are fundamental questions. The issue of the universal call to salvation is fundamental to the future of our dialogue. It is imperative that we, both Jews and Christians, have a mutual understanding of this vocation.

Seventh are the types of dialogue in which we need to be engaged. Our theological dialogue needs to have several levels. (Any dialogue that is carried out must be theological.) Cardinal Kasper has tried to encourage first and foremost a dialogue of life. I believe that *Nostra aetate* no. 2 encourages this level where Jews and Christians reflect theologically on their lives. What is our attitude and way of acting as we each witness to our faith? Here, key biblical concepts come to the fore, such as hospitality, justice, mercy, respect, and so forth. These spiritual realities need to be incarnated not only in our relationships with one another, but also with the whole of creation. This dimension of our theological dialogue should bear witness to our fidelity to the faithful God of our Fathers and Lord Jesus Christ.

A second level to the theological dialogue is that of action. *Nostra aetate* no. 3 speaks of the need to "preserve and promote peace, liberty, social justice, and moral values." The goal is to take us out of ourselves in concern for the common good. In other words, it is the exercise of making space for the other. Respect for the other, taken together with concern for the promotion of the common moral good, is an essential element of this dialogue.

A third level of dialogue deals with religious experience. This delves into deeper, spiritual dimensions. Here, it is our hope that through contemplation and ways of searching for the Absolute we will together be able to encounter the All Holy, the truly Other.

We must keep before our eyes that this is a dialogue of two historical faith communities. We do indeed share very much in common, but in many respects we have lost a common language. In spite of this fact, for some unknown reason, we have not explored our interrelationships. Could it be that we are afraid to divest ourselves and become "lesser brothers" to each other so that a space is found for the other in our lives? Are we afraid to share the knowledge that we have gained of the Holy One of Israel by different paths? Are we afraid of the responsibility we will have to bear for humanity in the created world? Despite our fears, the future of Jewish-Christian dialogue will ultimately depend on our "finding a place for the Other."

Afterword

Gregory Baum
Professor Emeritus and Theological Adviser to the
Secretariat for Christian Unity
at Vatican II

The fortieth anniversary of *Nostra aetate*, the Second Vatican Council's declaration that redefined the Catholic Church's teaching on Judaism and the Jewish people, is an event worthy of celebration. The promotion of Jewish-Christian dialogue and friendship is a cause that deserves the support of universities, the training ground of intellectuals who as teachers raise people's awareness and influence the public culture. I am honoured by the invitation to write an Afterword reflecting on the six essays found in this book, which offer a better understanding of *Nostra aetate* and its impact on Catholic-Jewish dialogue and friendship.

With many Catholics and Jews, I am grateful to Pope John XXIII, who decided to make the renewal of Catholic-Jewish relations a topic to be treated at the Second Vatican Council. I remember the first meeting of the Secretariat for Promoting Christian Unity, held in Rome in November 1960, when Cardinal Bea announced that John XXIII had asked that the Secretariat prepare a statement on Catholic-Jewish relations. (We found out much later that the Pope's decision had been influenced by a visit from the Jewish scholar Jules Isaac, about whom I shall say a few words further on.)

George Tavard's excellent essay in this volume describes the difficulties the Secretariat had in persuading the bishops at the Council of the new respect for Jews and Judaism. Strong support for this new openness was given by the American and Canadian bishops. Tavard also shows that, because of contrasting points of view, the original proposal of the Secretariat had to be somewhat modified. Still, its substantive message was preserved. The Council recognized the ongoing validity of God's Covenant with the first-chosen people, honoured the faith of contemporary Jews, and repudiated the discourse of contempt that had infiltrated the Christian tradition almost from the beginning. I understood *Nostra aetate* to say that since God's saving Word continues to sustain the Synagogue, the Church has no mission to convert Jews to Christianity.

Tavard's essay demonstrates that the new Catholic teaching was a properly theological proposal, not a diplomatic concession to modern pluralism. Rereading the Scriptures after the Holocaust made Christians hear the message of Saint Paul in Romans 11, to which no attention was paid in the traditional reading. The Apostle argues that while Israel, the chosen people, has on the whole refused to accept its messiah, Israel has not been rejected by God, because "the gifts and the call of God are irrevocable" (Rom 11:28). The promises of God continue to accompany this people.

Allow me to add that the rereading of Scripture in the light of new historical events is the appropriate theological method followed in the doctrinal renewal of the Church. John XXIII and John Paul II referred to this as listening to "the signs of the times." This method allows the Church to hear God's Word in a new way, revise previous interpretations, and discover the relevance of divine revelation for the conditions of the present.

Ovey Mohammed's informative essay on the Vatican's post-conciliar teaching on Jews and Judaism shows that the new thinking has been carried forward and offers replies to questions not clarified in the conciliar declaration. His essay summarizing the new teaching deserves to be read several times. I acquainted myself with these documents when they were first published, yet upon reading Mohammed's summary of the important points made by them, I am truly astounded. These are messages that have been largely ignored, even in the Catholic theological community.

It deserves to be mentioned that the Vatican now recognizes the fateful role played by the Church's anti-Jewish discourse in the spread of modern, racially based anti-Semitism that culminated in the Holocaust.

Remarkable also is that the new Catholic teaching honours the Jewish interpretation of Scripture and the faith of post-biblical Judaism. While the Church reads the Old Testament in the light of its fulfillment in Jesus Christ, the new Catholic teaching respects the different reading of Scripture made by the Synagogue. The question emerges whether both readings can be true. Are there two valid divine Covenants, as suggested generations ago by the Jewish religious philosopher Franz Rosenzweig? That there are two Covenants and two divine missions was suggested in a recent paper by Cardinal Walter Kasper.[1] At the same time, Christians and Jews confess that there are – and will ever be – substantive differences between them. How can these differences be reconciled? In his essay, Cardinal Cassidy quotes a sentence from the Jewish text *Dabru Emet* – about which more will be said later – proposing that "the humanly irreconcilable difference between Jews and Christianity ... will not be settled until God redeems the entire world as promised in the Scripture."[2] The Vatican *Guidelines* of 1976, as reported in Mohammed's essay, adopt a similar

---

1   Mohammed's essay, p. 68.
2   Cardinal Cassidy's essay, p. 106.

eschatological perspective: the Church and Israel together await God's final manifestation at the end of time.[3]

Cardinal Edward Cassidy was for many years President of the Pontifical Council for Promoting Christian Unity as well as President of the Vatican's Commission for Religious Relations with the Jews. His essay presents a hopeful picture of the future of Catholic-Jewish friendship, based on the many experiences in various parts of the world that have fostered dialogue and co-operation between Catholics and Jews. In his essay he reports many of these interreligious conferences and shows the remarkable progress that has been made. At high-level meetings of well-informed Catholics and Jews there is an abundance of goodwill, a readiness to live respectfully side by side and work together in common educational and cultural projects. At this level, the Jewish and Christian participants experience an embracing solidarity based on their common faith in the one God. Cardinal Cassidy recognizes that Catholics and Jews indifferent to theological issues – possibly representing the majority – are as yet unaware of the changed relationship between Catholics and Jews at the high level, even if suspicion, resentment, and hostility between the two communities have subsided. What is greatly needed – and demanded by all the contributors to this book – is an educational outreach to ordinary Christian and Jewish

---

3   Mohammed's essay, p. 56.

citizens, informing them of the teaching of *Nostra aetate* and the positive Jewish responses to it.

Since none of the authors mention the efforts of the Canadian Catholic Church to promote Catholic-Jewish dialogue and cooperation, I wish to recall two important initiatives.[4] In 1977, the Canadian Conference of Catholic Bishops (CCCB) joined the Canadian Council of Churches (CCC) and the Canadian Jewish Congress to form the Canadian Christian Jewish Consultation (CCJC). This liaison committee meets four or five times a year to discuss such practical issues as refugees and immigration, famine relief in Africa, and proselytism on university campuses. In partnership with the Newman Centre at the University of Toronto, the CCJC has sponsored symposia inviting Jewish, Christian, and Muslim reflection on such topics as The Spiritual Significance of Jerusalem, The Spiritual Significance of Suffering, The Meaning of Holiness and Virtue, and What Is at the Heart of Faith? In 1999, the CCJC produced a Yom Kippur liturgy for use by Christians in the year 2000. Since 2001, the CCJC has felt the impact of events in the Middle East, and members have engaged in some very serious conversations.

---

4   The following information was given to me by Sister Donna Geernaert, who worked for many years at the CCCB fostering Jewish-Christian relations. She is now the president of the Sisters of Charity located in Halifax, Nova Scotia.

Noteworthy also is that in 2000, the CCCB's Commission for Ecumenism developed a statement on Jewish-Catholic relations entitled *Jubilee: Renewing Common Bonds with the Jewish Community*. In October of that year, the document was released at the annual plenary assembly of the CCCB. At that occasion, the morning prayer was adapted from the Yom Kippur liturgy and Rabbi Howard Joseph of Montreal addressed the bishops and the observers. The statement was well received by the Jewish community in Canada and by a wide public in Israel.

A positive Jewish response to the new Catholic teaching is expressed in Professor David Novak's remarkable essay, which will amaze many readers. But before I turn to the Jewish response in this volume, I wish to mention the prehistory of *Nostra aetate* – that is to say, the movement in the Catholic Church prior to the Council that promoted Jewish-Christian reconciliation. To my knowledge, the history of this movement has never been written. After the emergence of Nazi anti-Semitism in the 1930s, prior to the Holocaust, a few Christian scholars recognized and lamented the anti-Judaism implicit in much of Christian preaching. The names I remember are Erik Peterson of Germany, James Parkes of England, Jacques Maritain of France, and Charles Journet of Switzerland.[5] In

---

5   Erik Petersen, *Die Kirche aus Juden und Heiden* (Salzburg: A Pustet, 1933); James Parkes, *The Conflict of the Church and the Synagogue: A Study in the Origin of Antisemitism* (London: Soncino Press, 1934); Jacques Maritain, *Antisemitism* (London: G. Bles, Centenary Press, 1939) and *A Christian Looks at the Jewish*

1947, when World War II had ended and the horror of the Holocaust had been revealed, a group of Christians, Catholics and Protestants, met at Seelisberg in Switzerland to face up to the anti-Jewish bias in passages of the New Testament and subsequent Christian preaching and to formulate a set of recommendations addressed to the churches for correcting these expressions of contempt.

Present at this meeting was a French Jewish historian, Jules Isaac, whose research and activity were to have a profound influence on the Catholic Church. There exists as yet no biography of this remarkable man. Hiding in French villages during the war, Jules Isaac had been able to survive, while his wife and daughter were arrested at home and sent to their deaths. He asked himself this anguished question: Where does this blind hatred of the Jews come from? Studying the New Testament, he detected in it passages that vilified the Jews who refused to believe in Jesus and expressed contempt for their religious practice. He entered into dialogue with Christian friends and in 1948 founded with them and some Jewish friends the association *Amitié judéo-chrétienne*. In the same year he published his influential book *Jésus et Israël*, which revealed in detail the teaching of contempt implicit in Christian preaching. Among the Catholics influenced by this book

---

Question (Toronto: Longmans, Green, 1939); and Charles Journet, *Destinées d'Israël* (Paris: Egloff, 1945).

were the priests and the sisters of our Lady of Sion in France, who soon dedicated themselves to wrestle against Christian anti-Jewish bias and promote Catholic-Jewish understanding. One of their priests, Paul Démann, edited the review *Cahier sioniens*, which emphasized the common heritage of Christians and Jews and proposed theological ideas, such as the abiding validity of the Mosaic Covenant, which anticipated the teaching of *Nostra aetate*. Jules Isaac remained committed to Jewish-Christian dialogue. In 1960, he went to see Pope John XXIII. During their conversation, the Pope promised that the Vatican Council would publish a text to reform and renew Catholic-Jewish relations.

Another part of the prehistory of *Nostra aetate* is the passionate engagement of Gertrud Luckner for the purification of Christian teaching and the theological solidarity between Christians and Jews.[6] During the war, she – a Catholic social worker at the time – was sent by her bishop to help Jews in hiding and other dissidents. She was arrested in 1943, spent the rest of the war in the notorious Ravensbrück concentration camp, and upon her release dedicated herself to the promotion of Jewish-Christian friendship. In 1948 she founded the review *Freiburger Rundbrief*, which brought into conversation Catholics, Protestants, and Jews who were critical of the

---

6   Luckner's story is told in Hans-Josef Wollasch, *Gertrud Luckner* (Freiburg im Breisgau: Herder, 2005).

past, yet stirred by theological hope. I met Gertrud Luckner in the mid-1950s; two participants of her circle included the Protestant theologian Karl Thieme and the Jewish historian Lutz Ehrlich. Like *Cahiers sioniens*, Gertrud Luckner's review proposed a new Christian approach that would eventually be endorsed by the conciliar teaching of Vatican II.

Professor David Novak's essay is a perfect gem. Reading it, one cannot help but be deeply moved by the author's faith, understanding, and generosity. He tells us that he was greatly impressed by the new teaching of *Nostra aetate*. If the Catholic Church has redefined its relationship to Jews and Judaism and now respects God's Covenant with the people of Israel, should not believing Jews, he asks himself, also rethink their relationship to Christianity? With three other Jewish theologians, he decided to publish a statement entitled *Dabru Emet* ("To speak the truth"), which recognizes the Church's new teaching and articulates an appreciation of Christianity from a Jewish point of view. In his essay, Novak expresses a Jewish respect for Christianity with a clarity and generosity that I have never read anywhere else. He recognizes that the Church sees itself as the new people of God, the fulfillment of the scriptural promises, and that this belongs to the substance of Christian faith that can never change. He then adds that Jews have no reason to be offended by this supersessionist teaching as long as it is not used as a theological motive for trying to convert Jews. The Jews themselves are faithful to their own religious tradition, which contradicts Christian doctrine. Jews and Christians are able to respect their differences without attempting to persuade one another to change their allegiance. Since there are no human resources for resolving the truth question, believers in both communities patiently leave the answer to God's final revelation at the end of history.

Novak argues that there is no reason for Jews to be angry that the Catholic Church accepts converts from Judaism, since the Jews themselves receive converts from Christianity. He recognizes, of course, that the Church's mission to convert Jews to the Christian faith profoundly insulted the Jewish community. Now the Church has changed its teaching. Because *Nostra aetate* and subsequent Vatican documents acknowledge that God's Word is celebrated in the Synagogue, the mission to convert Jews has lost its theological justification. Despite their doctrinal differences, Novak argues, Jews and Christians, urged by the common faith in the one God, can stand together in solidarity and explore ways of working together in the service of the common good. Very special in Novak's essay is the tone of friendship that pervades it.

At the same time, I am glad that the second Jewish speaker points to the tensions that continue to exist between Catholics and Jews. Riccardo Di Segni, the Chief Rabbi of Rome, recognizes the changes in the Church's official teaching, yet he is not convinced that *Nostra aetate* promises to end the Church's mission to convert the Jews. He is troubled by the discourse of John Paul II in praise of Edith Stein, Jewish convert and Carmelite nun, murdered at Auschwitz; and he worries about doctrinal statements made by Benedict XVI that continue to present the Church as the true Israel, the Israel of God, possibly implying that the first-chosen people are now the false Israel. Rabbi di Segni also refers to recent instances where priests have encouraged Jews to become Christians.

What Rabbi di Segni does not say, but which must have been on his mind, is the apostasy of Israel Zolli, Chief Rabbi of Rome, who decided in 1945 to become a Roman Catholic. According to the *Encyclopedia Judaica*, Rabbi Israel Zolli (Zoller) abandoned his congregation when the Germans entered Rome in 1943 and took refuge in the Vatican. After the war, rejected by the Jewish community because of his unworthy behaviour at a time of great danger, he became a Catholic and started an academic career in Italy.

Catholics, Protestants, and Jews living in pluralistic societies are grateful when their faith allows them to embrace pluralism and respect religious communities other than their own. Catholics in North America rejoiced in the new teaching of the Second Vatican Council because it allowed them to feel at home in their religiously pluralistic society. Protestants and Jews in North America were also glad that Catholics were now reconciled to pluralism. But the reaction of religious minorities in Catholic countries has been different. During the Council, I became friends with Paolo Ricca, a young theologian of the

Italian Waldensian Church, which had been persecuted and later marginalized by the Catholic Church from the eleventh century on. This loving and honest man found it almost impossible to believe the conciliar statement that honoured Protestants and recognized a spiritual union with them in the same faith. Who can be surprised that the Waldensians regarded the conciliar documents as diplomatic statements made by the authorities that would not change the Church's exclusionary attitude and behaviour at the community level? The very architecture of the Vatican and St. Peter's Church impresses dissidents as a princely palace, part baroque castle, part medieval fortress, symbolizing power. Who can be surprised that the Jewish community in Rome, living under the shadow of this giant monument, will be cautious in its reaction to promises made in a conciliar statement? Rabbi di Segni does not reject dialogue, but he is more interested in seeing changing attitudes and behaviour on the ground. His is a voice that deserves attention.

Father James Puglisi also works in Rome. He is the Minister General of the Franciscan Friars of the Atonement. He is active at the Centro Pro Unione, an ecumenical forum for research, teaching, and interreligious dialogue. Among the visitors are Jews concerned with improving Jewish-Christian relations. In his essay, Puglisi expresses a certain frustration that some of the representatives of large Jewish organizations he meets have a secular understanding of being Jewish and are not interested in matters of faith. This lack of symmetry marks a good number of Christian-Jewish encounters where the Christians wrestle with issues of faith and divine revelation and the Jews are simply preoccupied with restraining currents of anti-Semitism. While this may be frustrating, it is not at all surprising. Christians define themselves in religious terms, while Jews see themselves as a people or an ethno-cultural community. When Jews lose their faith in God, they continue to think of themselves as 100 per cent Jewish. Most of my Jewish friends are not religious at all – nor, to be honest, are they thrilled that the Catholic Church has learned to honour and appreciate contemporary Judaism. They are content with pluralism, friendship, and freedom.

Puglisi tells us that as a Franciscan he has a religious respect for "the Other" – the marginalized, the excluded, the despised. This message of Jesus, largely forgotten by the Church, is repeatedly reclaimed by her saints and prophets, especially Saint Francis of Assisi. Yet speaking of "the Other" is not part of the traditional theological vocabulary. References to *l'altérité* or otherness are recent. What Puglisi has in mind is not the otherness postulated by postmodern thought that denies any sharing across cultural boundaries. He relies, rather, on respect for otherness in the thought of Martin Buber and Emmanuel Lévinas, which extends solidarity to every person one encounters, however different he or she may be. Puglisi's vocabulary reminds me of the great influence modern Jewish thinkers have had on Christian theology. Buber and Lévinas, each in his own way, found, in the encounter with the Other, an entry into metaphysics and a signal of divine presence. Their writings are studied in Christian theological faculties. Franz Rosenzweig's idea of the two Covenants, later defended in Canada by Rabbi Günther Plaut, was picked up by Paul Démann, editor of *Cahiers sioniens*, and, more recently, raised as a question by Walter Kasper.[7] Emil Fackenheim had a great influence on Christian thinking in Canada. I am grateful to David Novak for recalling the life and thought of Abraham Joshua Heschel, whose prophetic interpretation of Scripture deeply moved his many Christian readers. The recent book *The Political Theology of Paul*, written by the Jewish philosopher Jacob Taubes, is read by Christians with excitement. The surprising affinity between contemporary Jewish and Christian theological reflection is brought about by their common wrestling with the insights and errors of modern thought.

None of the essays in this book mentions the shadow that the Israeli-Palestinian conflict has cast on Jewish-Christian relations. Perhaps the contributors think that this is a political matter that has nothing to do with the substantive issues of religion and theology. Yet there are Jewish religious thinkers who hold different views. Some of them defend the expansionist policies of the Jewish State on religious grounds,

---

7   See footnote 1 above.

invoking the full extent of God's gift of the Land to the chosen people, while others oppose Israel's prolonged occupation of Palestine and the Jewish settlements on confiscated territory as contrary to the ethics of Judaism and violations of international law. Prominent among the latter are two critical peace groups in Israel that oppose the government on theological grounds: Rabbis for Human Rights[8] and the Orthodox association Oz VeShalom.[9] In the United States, prominent is Rabbi Michael Lerner, editor of the magazine *Tikkun* and founder of the nationwide Tikkun Community.[10] There exists a significant amount of Jewish literature that supports the State of Israel but strongly opposes its policies regarding the Palestinians.[11]

There is no denying that the Christian churches, including the Vatican, are in anguish over the Israeli-Palestinian conflict. Remembering with repentance their age-old anti-Jewish rhetoric, the churches hesitate to criticize the Jewish State; at the same time, their regret over their former identification with the colonial powers has generated solidarity with the

---

8   www.rhr.israel.net

9   www.netivot-shalom.org.il/index.php

10   www.tikkun.org

11   Two recent books are Tony Kushner and Alisa Slomon, eds., *Wrestling with Zion: Progressive Jewish-American Responses to the Israeli-Palestinian Conflict* (New York: Grove Press, 2003) and Adam Shatz, ed., *Prophets Outcast: Dissenting Jewish Writings about Zionism and Israel* (New York: Nation Books, 2004).

anti-colonial struggles in the developing world and created a special sympathy for the Palestinians.[12] Every church deals with this malaise in its own way, often preferring silence.

It would be a tragic mistake if the shadow of the Israeli-Palestinian conflict were allowed to inhibit theological dialogue and co-operative ventures between Christians and Jews. *Jews and Catholics Together*, in commemorating the fortieth anniversary of *Nostra aetate*, demonstrates that commitment to mutual respect and interreligious friendship is founded upon divine revelation and thus is capable of transcending historical differences. Listening to their sacred texts, Jews and Christians hear the divine summons that renews the understanding of their tradition and makes them more faithful to the Covenant that created them.

---

12 Gregory Baum, "Jewish-Christian Dialogue under the Shadow of the Israeli-Palestinian Conflict," *Théologiques* (Special issue entitled *Juifs et chrétiens. L'avenir du dialogue*) 11 (2003): 205–222.

APPENDIX[1]

*Questions Concerning the Jews:
Proposals from the Secretariat for Christian Unity
November 1961*

Introduction

In his Epistle addressed "to all God's beloved in Rome" (Rom. 1:7), St. Paul discusses Christ, in whom the fullness of God's love resides, and proclaims him to be the one source of our justification. These ideas compel St. Paul, as it were, to reflect on the mystery of God's providence towards Israel (ch. 9–10).

As these chapters show, the Apostle is affected by both sadness and joy. He is saddened because so many who are his "kinsmen by race" (9:3) remain far from Christ; but he rejoices since, despite their parting, God does not reject the

---

[1] Translated by Marc B. Cels

people whom he had formerly chosen. Preaching that Israel from whom Christ is descended will at last return to the Lord "so that all of Israel shall be saved" (11:26), the Apostle exclaims: "I want you to understand this mystery, brethren" (11:25). Explaining this passage, Thomas Aquinas notes that, "Ignorance of this mystery is harmful for us."[2]

These words of the Angelic Doctor can be connected without any difficulty to the other works of God involving all the offspring of Abraham's loins. These works will encourage Christians to remember a more friendly coexistence with the Jews. For when Christians recognize in their minds and hearts the intimate relationship in faith that they once had with the Jews, consider their bond of love that still exists with the Jews in our time, even if they are yet separated from Christ and the Church, and when they preserve the hope of the ultimate union with the Jews, they vividly recall God's mercy and faithfulness. And in recalling the Lord's mercy, Christians are grateful to God on account of his great glory, and thus their "youth will be renewed like the eagle's" (Ps 103:5 [Vg Ps 102:5]).

---

[2] Thomas Aquinas, "Commentary on the Letter to the Romans," caput XI, lectio IV, ad 11,25 in *Opera Omnia* Vol. XX (Paris: Vivès, 1876): 542.

1. The Church's Roots in the Old Testament

Anyone truly wishing to understand the Church should acknowledge that it is just like the spouse of Christ, and his body, the people of God, the communion of the faithful. Therefore, in order that the mystery of the Church may be properly understood, it is proper to pay as much attention as possible to those roots that the Church has in the life and faith of the ancient Hebrews.

St. Augustine taught that God's call and Abraham's response was a "turning point in time."[3] Indeed, it was then that a new age of faith in the living and true God was born. For this reason the text of the Roman Pontifical does not hesitate to call the life of the Patriarch "the seed of our faith."[4] St. Augustine also affirmed that it was not just one man or another, but also the whole Israelite people who were the prophets of the Messiah and his kingdom.[5] The sacred liturgy often celebrates the Exodus of Israel from Egypt and the other mighty deeds of God as true elements in the history of Holy Church. Indeed, the Easter Proclamation says, "This

---

3 Augustine of Hippo, "City of God," 12, in *Patrologiae cursus completes, Series Latina*, Vol. XLI (Paris: Garnier, 1844-): 492.

4 "De Altaris Consecratione," in *Pontificale Romanum: Summorum Pontificum Iussu Editum a Benedicto XIV et Leone XIII, Pontificibus Maximus Recognitum et Castigatum* (Malines: H. Dessain, 1958).

5 Augustine of Hippo, "Against Faustus," 13,4, in *Patrologiae cursus completes, Series Latina*, Vol. XLII (Paris: Garnier, 1844-): 283.

is the night in which you first brought forth our forefathers, the Children of Israel, out of Egypt, and led them dry-shod through the Red Sea."

Therefore, no one strays from the truth by saying that Israel of the Patriarchs and Prophets is the Church in its beginning or the seed of the Church; yet the Church is Israel fulfilled, purified by the blood of Christ and spread through the whole world. Old Israel is the origins of the Church, and the Church truly is Israel transformed by the word of Christ and renewed by the fire of the Holy Spirit.

Indeed, although the two Testaments differ between themselves, one never contradicts the other; rather, they are two steps in God's one communication to humankind. There is no doubt that the New surpasses the Old. But to undervalue the Israelite lineage and the old dispensation, as is happening again, is unjust and therefore disgraces Christ himself, who wished to be born from that lineage. God's plan is one and undivided and the economy of salvation is one and undivided. Because of this, Holy Church prays, "that the fullness of the whole world may pass on to the sons of Abraham and the Israelite dignity."[6]

---

6 "Easter Vigil Liturgy," in *Missale Romanum. Ex Decreto Sacrosancti Concilii Tridentini Restitutum. Summorum Pontificum Cura Recognitum. Editio VIII Juxta Editionem VI Post Typicam Vaticanam* (Boston: Benzinger Bros., 1956).

First Recommendation

Let it be moved:

- that the Church's roots already appeared, according to God's plan, in Israel of the Patriarchs and Prophets;
- that the call of Abraham and the Exodus of the chosen people from Egypt pertain to the origins of the Church and the start of her history;
- that the Church is a living continuation of the people of God living under the old dispensation and is Israel renewed and enriched by the word and blood of Christ.

2. The Jews Are Forever Beloved by God

Because of the great hatred and many quarrels among humankind that today still sunder the human race, the universality of the Church must be emphasized. Indeed this universality embraces the Jews and the Gentiles within one love.

According to the thought of St. Paul, the division of the human race into Jews and Gentiles and their reconciliation are of the greatest importance. In Christ this wound is healed, as the Apostle rejoices, "For he is our peace, who has made us both one and has broken down the dividing wall of hostility… in his flesh" (Eph. 2:14). This inner healing is the sign of divine love embracing all people or rather it is also the sign of our salvation that should shine out before the world.

By the preaching of Christ the people of Israel are divided; for not all accept the word of the Gospel. The leaders of the people asked for the death of the Lord; however "a remnant, chosen by grace" (Rom. 11:15) followed him faithfully. From among these, the early Church was constituted; they, and chiefly the Holy Apostles and the Blessed Virgin Mary, gave the rule for all future Christian life.[7]

Alas, sadly, some of those in Jerusalem at that time shouted before Pilate, "His blood be upon us and our children" (Matt. 27:25) but in the same Jerusalem, where the first crowd raged, "there followed him a great multitude of the people and of women who bewailed and lamented him" (Lk 23:27). Later on, however, the residents of Jerusalem, ignorant of the time of the visitation and that the Lord Christ was offering peace, were punished by the great destruction of the Temple and the City of the great King (cf. Lk 12:49-53).

It must also be noted that St. Paul, when he speaks about his kindred who did not know Christ Jesus, deliberately applies the word *paraptōma*, i.e. "stumble", and the word *eptaisan*, that is, "trespass" (cf. Rom. 11:11-12). On the contrary, as he says, his kinsmen by race, even if they resist the plan of salvation, nevertheless remain most dear to God (Rom. 11:28). Beloved

---

[7] Charles Journet, *Destinées d'Israël* (Paris: Egloff, 1945), 112.

for the sake of their forefathers, they unknowingly witnessed to the gracious will of God towards all people, manifested in Christ Jesus.

Cardinal Achilles Liénart wrote with this understanding in the *Litteris Pastoralibus* at Easter of 1960. He affirms here that it is not proper that Christians consider the Jews an accursed people, a mob of deicides who merit our hatred; on the contrary, he declares that the sins of all humankind, not only those of the Jews, were the cause of the Lord's death. "Truly, the religious destiny of the Israelite people is a mystery of grace, which all of us Christians should contemplate within our hearts reverently and sympathetically."[8]

Second Recommendation

Let it be moved:

- that Christ, our peace, united Jews and Gentiles in his Church;
- that their reconciliation is a figure of the reconciliation of the whole earth in the Church;
- that the Jewish people, although separated from Christ, are not accursed, but remain most beloved to God, on account of their forefathers and the promises given to them.

---

8 "La question juive et la conscience chrétienne," *La Documentation Catholique* 1323 (6 March 1960): cols. 299–300.

3. The Final Reconciliation of the Synagogue with the Church

At the time of the apostles, the race of Israel was divided. The smaller part, "a remnant chosen by grace," was the source out of which the universal Church was formed, to be spread through the whole world; the larger part, however, even if unbelieving, nevertheless was preserved as a surety of God's mercy and faithfulness (Rom. 11:30-32). The Apostle praises God's faithful and superabundant mercy, "For the gifts and the call of God are irrevocable" (Rom. 11:29). Therefore, the race of Israel, now separated from Christ, will be restored in communion with him on the appointed day. The Church firmly holds this hope that Israel will be reconciled.

How Israel is to be reconciled and what the first fruits of this reconciliation will be are unknown to us. Theodore of Mopsuestia thought that the Jews of those days will fervently announce the Christian faith.[9] St. Gregory the Great asserted that they will bear reproaches and torture in imitation of the suffering Christ.[10] Photius wrote that the reconciliation of the Jewish people will bring "a perfect and universal joy" to everyone, a perfect life and the resurrection of the dead.[11]

---

9 Cf. Karl Staab, *Pauluskommentare: aus der griechischen Kirche aus Katenenhandschriften* (Münster: Aschendorff, 1933), 156.

10 Gregory the Great, in *Patrologiae cursus completes, Series Latina*, Vol. LXXIX (Paris: Garnier, 1844-): 108.

11 Cf. Staab, *Pauluskommentare*, 526.

Origen was of the opinion that, through that reconciliation, this corruptible world will be made incorruptible.[12]

Even though many things about how Israel will be received remain uncertain, nevertheless the hope for the reconciliation of Israel is essentially affirmed in Holy Scripture (cf. Rom. 11:12, 15, and 25).[13] For it is a divine promise, an apostolic inheritance, an expectation of the Church that is never to be extinguished until it be done.

Third Recommendation

Let it be moved:

- that the reconciliation of the Jewish people with the Church is an integral part of Christian hope;
- that the Church with unshakable faith and a great desire, hopes for the return of this people;
- that the Church, although it does not know the day or hour of this return, knows with the Apostle, however, that this will be an event filled with grace, or rather "life out of death."

---

12 Origen, in *Patrologiae cursus completes, Series Graeca*, Vol. XIV (Paris: Migne, 1857-): 1190–1191.

13 "De antisemitismo vitando," in *Acta et Documenta Concilio Oecumenico Vaticano II Apparando*, Series I, Vol. IV, Pars I, pp. 131, 344–345.

4. The Jews Are Our Separated Kinsmen

By the decree of divine providence the two testaments are united by a perfect succession. The sons of the Church are joined together with the sons of Israel both in hope and also in sadness, as the Apostle declares (Rom. 9:12). Because of this, but especially because of the invincible fidelity of God towards the Jewish people, out of love for the elect, Christians should feel nothing other than admiration and love towards the sons of Abraham. Even if they are separated from each other by faith, Christians regard the Jews as kinsmen, because they are the race of Christ.

This was the understanding of Pius XI when he rejected antisemitism by insisting that Abraham, progenitor of the Jewish people, was also father of the faith of all Christians. "Spiritually," he said, "we are Semites."[14] And John XXIII, clearly implying the bonds of fraternity, greeted some among the Jews in this way: "I am Joseph, your brother" (Gen. 45:4). Indeed, he indicated that those who only accept the Old Testament are far away from those who also acknowledge the new and the supreme rule; they are separated, but remain brothers. "We are all sons of the heavenly Father; among us all radiant love must be kept and cultivated."[15]

---

14 "Address to Belgian Pilgrims," *La Documentation Catholique* 885 (5 December 1938): col. 1460.

15 Cf. *L'Osservatore Romano* (October 19, 1960).

Holy Church deeply shuns all racism and especially, as much as possible, antisemitism. Both are opposed not only to truth, justice, and charity, but also offend against faith. All hatred is contrary to divine revelation that teaches that all humankind is created in God's image. Anti-Semitism however is worse since it deplores, at least implicitly, the fact that when the Word of God assumed flesh he became the son of David and the son of Abraham (Matt. 1:1).

Fourth Recommendation

Let it be moved:

- that every person is worthy of love, having been created in the image and likeness of God;
- that racism is the gravest danger of our age, since it shatters the bond of love between brethren;
- that antisemitism is a sin not only against justice, charity, and the bond of fraternity, but also against Jesus Christ, who became man from out of the House of David.